BETWEEN THE *flowers* AND THE BROKEN

STORIES, SONGS, AND LESSONS
FROM THE STREETS OF BRAZIL

NIC BILLMAN

Foreword by Randy Clark

Unless otherwise identified, Scripture quotations are taken from the New King James Version. Copyright © 1982 by Thomas Nelson, Inc. Used by permission. All rights reserved.

Shores of Grace Ministries
3677 Forte Road
Joelton, TN 37080
615-208-3845
www.shoresofgrace.com

Printed in the United States of America

ISBN-13: 978-0615799407
ISBN-10: 061579940X

I want to walk with You Papa,
Just a stroll through the garden,
The garden of life—
Between the flowers and the broken

.

Endorsements

When I first met the Billmans, I knew I was standing face-to-face with a company of God's Love Champions. They understand His heart. Not only have they embraced His heart, but they communicate His love with such authenticity as a family that is willing to lay down everything and serve the broken. They are willing to give their lives to revealing God's amazing and redeeming love to some of the most devastated in society.

I love and deeply respect the Billmans, and I love this book! As you read *Between the Flowers and the Broken*, you will be transformed. This book is for you; it is for us all. I wept, rejoiced, pondered, and received as I read through this wonderful communication born of the Spirit of God. I have truly been impacted and so will you.

Perhaps you will find yourself called to join the company of Love Champions who will take His love-light into the darkness, and you might even receive a specific call to the broken as you read through this book. One thing is for sure; the Spirit of God will introduce you to depths of His heart that will refresh, empower, and seal you in His love.

Oh how He loves you! Be filled with fresh revelation of His goodness and wonderful compassionate love—and then go and give it away.

Patricia King
www.xpmedia.com

Here is a book that will move you from pity to compassion. Instead of wringing your hands, you will be reaching your hands to the broken and outcast. Nic Billman shows us how to move from concern to connection. He takes us from the streets of Jerusalem with Jesus to Brazil, to our own streets. He takes us from admiring the work of the Son of God to ministering in the power of the Spirit as sons of God. When you read, have your traveling clothes on because you'll be heading out to write your own chapter. Nic Billman makes the life you've dreamed of seem possible. He makes the things you always wanted to do seem natural. He makes it so normal you will find yourself changing your plans. One minute we are walking with Jesus in the Galilean countryside and the next we are with Shores of Grace on the harsh streets of Brazil. And almost without notice your mind is envisioning your own streets and your own adventures with the healer from Nazareth. Read to your blessing and to your endangerment. Your comfort zone is about to be stretched. Your future is about to change.

Alan Hawkins
Founder & Senior Pastor, New Life City
Albuquerque, NM

One of the pleasures of reading Nic Billman's book *Between the Flowers and the Broken* is that his writing engages the real world. Using stories from both the Bible and the streets of Brazil, Nic helps us to see that compassion is part of the character of God and, therefore, should be part of the people of God's character as well. His definition, "compassion is love in action," becomes a challenge to every Christian everywhere.

This book reveals that Nic Billman has both the heart of a pastor and the mind of a practical theologian—a mix so greatly needed today in Brazil and around the world.

Nic begins his Closing Declaration by saying: "I pray this book has been a blessing and a challenge to you." To me, it certainly has. And I hope every Christian leader in Brazil will have both the opportunity and the pleasure of reading it.

Bishop João Carlos Lopes
Presiding Bishop, United Methodist Church of Brazil

Like many others, I fell in love with Nic before meeting him because he was singing my heart. It has been an honor to get to know Nic and his family. His passion for the Lord combined with his compassion for the least of these are so real and are revealed in this inspiring book.

In the book, Nic tells about a vision he had where he saw the Church alive and full of light crying out to see God's face and to hear His voice; then he saw the lost and the broken, and from their mouths he heard the voice of the Lord, "Then come find me." Nic was suddenly back in the Church, and the people were crying out, "We want to see Your face; we want to hear Your voice; we want to see You!" Quickly, he was back to the streets again, and the voice of the Lord again came from the broken, "Come find me." During a return trip to the U.S. this summer, I was at the airport reflecting on all that I had just experienced stateside. I was drawing near to the Lord, wanting to thank Him for everything I had just experienced and really just wanting Him. At that time, I just happened to be listening to Nic's song, "Come Find Me." I was flooded with emotion and fresh revelation that, in a few hours, I would be back home in China surrounded by the least of these, and yes, I would see Him! I share that story because to me that is an example of the impact of Nic's ministry, and in *Between the Flowers and the Broken*, Nic's love shines through his stories, songs, and lessons.

Mike Vant Hul
Co-founder and Co-director, Loaves and Fishes International
Hidden Treasures Home
Fuzhou, Fujian, China

Dedication

This book is dedicated to the men, women, and children trapped in prostitution and sex trafficking on the streets of Brazil. Our hearts are full of love and expectation for you, and we will never stop fighting for your destinies. One day soon, we will together bring the head of this giant called sex trafficking to the King of kings as an offering and a symbol of our victory.

Acknowledgements

To my best friend and amazing wife, Rachael, and to our four incredible children—no one has taught me as much as you. You inspire me to be who I was created to be.

To my parents and in-laws—thank you for being such amazing examples of compassion and love to Rachael and me, even in our weakest moments.

To our spiritual sons and daughters in Brazil—you have taught us so much about the love of the Father and have faithfully and lovingly gone with us to some of the darkest places in Brazil.

To Randy Clark, Patricia King, João Lopes, Alan Hawkins, and Mike and Deena Vant Hul—thank you for your kind words and encouragement.

Contents

Foreword

Between the Flowers and the Broken is Nic Billman's new book. I have to admit, when I heard Nic was writing a book, I was excited. I knew it would be a powerful book. And I was not disappointed when I read the insights and stories from Nic and Rachael's lives. When I first met Nic and Rachael, his wife, they were leading worship. I was so touched by the words of the songs they had written that I went home to tell my wife, DeAnne, about them and the power of the songs.

Nic and Rachael attended Global Awakening's school, The Global School of Supernatural Ministry, for two years. There was and is something special and unique about them. After graduating, they moved their family by faith to Brazil, where they now work among the prostitutes, transvestites, children, and teenagers who have been thrown out onto the streets. The power of their songs is reflected in the compassion of their lives. My wife has played their albums for about four years in our home, almost nonstop. I expected Nic's writing to carry this compassion and to tell of God's power. I was not disappointed. If you want to read a book that will open your eyes to the grace of Jesus, the love and acceptance of the Father, and the power of the Holy Spirit, then you should read *Between the Flowers and the Broken*. Let me suggest that, before you sit down to read, you have a box of tissues close by; you will need them.

My spiritual father, Jack Taylor, emphasizes the importance of the writer in regard to books. I agree. I don't want to read something written within someone's brain. I don't want to read someone's fiction; I want to read someone's story. I love it when fact is harder to believe than fiction. I love it when the story comes from life and is capable of breathing life into others. Nic Billman is one of my heroes of the faith. His whole family is an amazing example of faith, hope, and love—from his little daughter dancing on stage while Nic and Rachael lead worship to their complete comfort with prostitutes and transvestites. I know this family, I know their story, and I know their lives. This is a story that arises out of lives completely surrendered to God. This is a story where fact is harder to believe than fiction. This is the supernatural story of a young Methodist family who would bring great pride to John Wesley if he were alive today. It is time for the stories that, I believe, are known in Heaven to become known on the earth; it is time for the world to learn about *Between the Flowers and the Broken*.

—Randy Clark

Introduction

In the beginning, the Father created a Garden for His sons and daughters—
the original paradise called Eden, a place designed by the Creator for the
pleasure and dominion of His children. The Garden resonated with His
voice, and His footprints marked every path. There the Father would come
and call His children by name, inviting them to walk with Him in the cool
of the day. He delighted in them, and they delighted in Him.

In the midst of this beauty, one day, the serpent came and deceived
Adam and Eve. He convinced them to eat the fruit of the tree of the
knowledge of good and evil, the only forbidden tree in the Garden. This
one act caused sin to enter the world; consequentially, the children had to
leave the Garden. Ever since that day, sin, sickness, and brokenness have
marred the world. The footprints of God were no longer seen on the Earth.
The Father visited His children, but it was not the same. He could no longer
walk with His children through the Garden.

Many years later, on a starry night in a little city called Bethlehem,
Jesus the Messiah was born, and the footprints of God appeared once again
upon the Earth. Jesus walked upon the waves and the dirty streets alike.
He danced upon injustice, throwing the enemy under His feet. He was not
only the sacrifice but the model, too—doing only what He saw the Father
doing. He walked hand-in-hand with the Father through the garden of life.
Unlike the paradise of Eden, this garden was filled with brokenness. But
Jesus delighted in this garden just as the Father had delighted in Eden. He
loved the rejected and abused. He healed the sick. He cleansed the lepers.
He raised the dead and set the captives free. Although He walked among

the broken, He saw them with the eyes of the Father. Refusing to fixate on the circumstances and conditions of a fallen world, He saw with the eyes of destiny. Where the world saw a valley of dry bones, He saw an army. Where the world saw a funeral, He saw a wedding. Where the world saw a cemetery, He saw a garden. Although He walked among the broken, He saw the flowers. He spoke destiny and purpose— transforming lives with every step.

Jesus was the perfect model for the children of God. We are designed to follow His footprints through the garden. All creation groans and waits for the revealing of the children of God, for the unveiling of the true identities of the desperate and needy. The Father has hidden treasure among the lost, the sick, and the broken, and it is our privilege—our glory—to seek that treasure with Him (see Prov. 25:2). Once again, He is calling His sons and daughters by name, inviting us to walk with Him through the garden of life—between the flowers and the broken.

PART ONE

The Invitation

By Nic and Rachael Billman

I see the light coming from the throne
Breaking through the night as You call.
I feel the trembling
The trembling of the dark
At each mention of Your name,
Jesus, Jesus, Jesus.

Come up here, come up here,
My beloved, my bride.

I hear the cries, the cries of a broken bride
And I long to hold you in My arms
As we dance.
I've taken away
The stained and filthy rags that you once called identity.
And I have laid out garments of white
Sewn with grace and washed in blood.

Come up here, come up here,
My beloved, my bride.

The Spirit and the Bride say come.
The Spirit and the Bride say come.
The Spirit and the Bride say come.

CHAPTER ONE

Daddy, Can I Come?

For you did not receive the spirit of bondage again to fear,
but you received the Spirit of adoption by whom we cry out,
"Abba, Father."

—Romans 8:15

My daughter Leila is seven years old, and she is the apple of my eye. She is definitely a daddy's girl! When I'm home, she likes to be right by my side at all times, and when I'm away, she frequently asks my wife, Rachael, to call me so she can "say hi to Daddy." When I get home from a trip, she's usually waiting by the door. She knows the sound of my car, and she knows the sound of my footsteps. Before I make it to the door, she runs to me, jumps into my arms, and announces to the whole world, "Yay! Daddy's home!"

No matter what I'm going to do, Leila asks me, "Daddy, can I come?"

I'll say, "Okay, I'm running to the store real quick."

She'll say, "Daddy, can I come?"

Or I'll say, "I'm going to a meeting."

Still, she says, "Daddy, can I come?"

Or maybe it's, "I'm going to get something out of the car."

Even still, she chimes, "Daddy, can I come?"

Though the majority of our ministry is on the streets and in dangerous places, Leila still wants to come. In fact, our three oldest children ask at least once a week when they will be old enough to go to the streets with us. We haven't taken them yet to do street ministry at night, for their own safety. However, when we go to the favelas (slums) they come with us, and they play with the kids there, and they pray for the people. When we bring the street kids to our house or when our children go to visit the rescue homes, they love to play with the kids. Even though they know the streets are full of danger, they are not afraid because the perfect love of the Father casts out all fear (see 1 John 4:18). They want to be where their papa is. They see what their mom and dad do, and they want to be with us.

Not too long ago, I was worshipping at a park, just me and my guitar. I was thinking about Leila and her request, "Daddy, can I come," and the Holy Spirit said to me, "Nic, that is ministry." I began to cry at the beauty of this picture. Ministry is being with the Father and doing the things that He does. Ministry is lifting up our hands and saying, "Daddy, can I come? Where You go, I want to go. I won't be afraid because Your love casts out all fear. Here's my hand, Daddy. I want to go with You wherever You go."

You see, Leila understands that her identity is found within the eyes and the heart of her father. The way I look at her tells her she's special. The way I talk to her tells her she's valued, and the way I hold her tells her she is loved. She knows her daddy will care for her and protect her no matter what. That knowledge removes fear from her life—and our Father's love will do the same for us! That's the point of this book. When we know our identity in the Father and we're walking with Him, we don't have fear. Instead, we are able to extravagantly love the broken (just like He does) and tell them where they come from and who they really are. And in the times when fear does creep in, we simply grab the hand of our Papa, and we are strengthened by His touch.

Knowing the strength and nearness of our Papa, my wife, children, and I have dedicated our lives to rescuing the beautiful men, women, and children who are in bondage to prostitution and abuse. This book is a collection of stories, songs, and lessons that we have learned in our first two years walking the streets of Brazil. Along the way, we've realized that we are not very different than the people on the streets. We are all sons and daughters longing for the embrace of our Father. We're all standing at different stages on the journey, but the desire in our hearts makes us the same. We long for Papa. We long for the purpose for which we were created—intimacy with our Father. And He longs for us, too. This story is not just about the innate cry of our hearts to belong but also the crazy compassion of a Father who refuses to give up on His kids. We've found the Father and His Son on the streets, and it's changed everything for us.

How I Got My New Heart

But first, let's start at the beginning of this journey—the events God used to tell me I belong in Brazil. In 2008, I visited Brazil for the first time while traveling with Randy Clark as a student at his Global School For Supernatural Ministry. One day, at a retreat for the students, a Brazilian man named Gustavo Paiva—who has since become one of my best friends—taught. He started by saying, "As I'm teaching, I believe some of you will be called permanently to the nations."

I thought to myself, *How great! God is going to call some missionaries today. That's wonderful for **them**!*

Moments later, I found myself walking to the front of the room—all the while asking my legs why they were taking me there. Lying down on the ground, I immediately began to cry. For several hours I could not move under the weight of God's immense love. I didn't know what God was doing in my heart; all I could do was cry. That night, several friends helped me get on the bus and then to my hotel room. As I lay in bed, I asked the Father what He was doing in my heart; He didn't respond, and after a while, I fell asleep.

The next morning, God awakened me with these words, "I have given you a new heart, a heart for this nation and clarity of vision."

Before that day, Brazil had never been in my heart, much less on my mind, but for every day since that encounter, my heart has burned for our adopted nation. When I stepped out of the hotel that day, I saw every Brazilian as family, and my heart was forever changed.

The only problem is—I thought—*now I need to call Rachael and tell her that we are going to move to Brazil.*

With a bit of trepidation, I called her on Skype from the hotel lobby. "Hey Babe," I said, "I need to talk to you about something."

Her response left me speechless. "I know," she said. "We are moving to Brazil. Last night I had a vision of you lying on the ground crying, and I saw a clock spinning for several hours. The Lord asked me, 'If he calls you, will you say yes?' So my answer is yes."

On the same day, my older brother, Luke, while driving in Pennsylvania, saw a vision of poor and sick children in slums. He was so overtaken with compassion that he had to pull over as he wept and wept. He called me that day, forgetting that I was in Brazil, and although I had my cell service turned off, his call came through. When he shared the vision with me, I reminded him that I was in Brazil and told him that, *just that day,* I had seen a slum like the one he described.

A few days later, as I looked out the window of the bus I was riding, I saw many women prostituting on the streets. With my natural eyes, I saw each of their faces as the face of my daughter Leila. God broke my heart that night for his lost daughters who are trapped in prostitution, trafficking, and abuse. The life of our family has never been the same.

The Party Invitation

In the two years since that time, as we have gone to the streets of Brazil several times each week, we have encountered children who are far from home, far from God's plan for their lives. Prostitutes and transvestites calculate their value according to how much someone will pay to sleep with them. Women believe they deserve abuse. Children as young as eight sell their bodies for three dollars. Or for food or cigarettes. Or even just for credibility on the streets. Others of the same age smoke crack, drink alcohol, and sniff glue on a nightly basis. Some of our homeless friends are supremely talented artists who have lost their minds in alcoholism and drug addiction. And babies as young as three months old sometimes sleep on cardboard on the streets in some of the most dangerous sections of our city.

We know we're not the answer.

But we know who is.

We know where these lost children can find a home. See, all of their pain and sin started with one big problem—they don't know their Father. And because of that, they don't know who they are.

We Are Family

So many people think God is all about the rules, but He's not. He's about family. In fact, when He sent His Son to earth, He preached one simple message: "Your Father loves you! Repent and return to Him!" If God was about the rules, He probably would have sent a general to lead a great Christian army or an anointed politician to replace the worldly government with His. But He didn't because He was after something much deeper. He was re-establishing our original design—as children in His family. He was after our hearts.

We are the prize God sought when He sent Jesus to earth. We were the joy set before Jesus when He endured the cross (see Heb. 12:2). It was all for one purpose—to bring us back into the family. To that end, God sent His own Son to earth as a baby. As Isaiah 9:6 says, *"For unto us a Child is born, unto us a Son is given: and the government will be upon His shoulders..."* This was God's master plan—to send a baby boy and establish His everlasting government upon His shoulders. If we're thinking logically, it sounds like a joke. Who sends a child to win a kingdom? But God is no fool. And in fact, what He sent Jesus to win is not only a Kingdom, but a family. To understand, we must look back to God's original design at the beginning.

Walking in the Garden

In the Garden of Eden, before humanity's fall into sin, God walked with Adam and Eve in the cool of the day (see Gen. 3). This was God's original plan, a place where the Father and His children could dwell and commune together, a place where they could live face-to-face and heart-to-heart. This is still His desire.

So many of His children—like our friends on the streets of Brazil—don't know what they were made for or where they belong. They don't know their Father's name, but their hearts long for Him. Because they don't know what they're worth or how much He loves them, they've made some really bad choices. They've tried to satisfy that deep desire for the Father as best they could, but they have discovered only pain. God has a different plan, and He sent His son Jesus—and now us—to the streets to tell His lost kids about it. More than anything, He wants to walk with them through the garden of life.

Even in the Church, many of God's children don't know what they were created for. Many of us put a lot of emphasis on certain people, like pastors and prophets, expecting them to hear God for us. Certainly, God does frequently speak to His people through His people, and we should honor them and thank God for the spiritual leaders in our lives. But we should never seek out their voices in place of God's. He desires an intimate relationship with each of His children. The Garden of Eden had no judges, prophets, or kings, but just a Father and His children. Prophets, kings, and judges are all a part of God's redemptive plan, but they were not part of His *original* plan.

Many people keep themselves busy running around to church services, conferences, and retreats—seeking to hear a word from God through a pastor, prophet, or speaker. All the while, they forget that they can hear His voice, too. In God's grace, He will communicate to us through events and other people. But sometimes the Father sits on the porch, as we're running out the door to the next event, and says, "My children, slow down. I'm right here. Let's take a walk together."

This is His invitation to everyone of us, in every situation of life. Whether we're rich or poor, whether we're upstanding citizens or those of low repute, His desire for us is the same. "Come, let's walk the streets of life together; let's plant flowers along the sidewalks."

Morning by Morning

Here's the amazing thing: The creator of the universe is with me, and He wants to be my friend. He wants to talk to me and to hear what I have to say. We can get so used to biblical words and ideas that we forget how incredible they really are. Just think about that—*the Creator of the Universe wants to take a walk with me!*

I am so thankful that "*...He awakens me morning by morning, He awakens my ear to hear as the learned*" (Isa. 50:4). I am so thankful that He speaks to each of us every day. (If we don't know how to listen, we may not recognize His voice, but He is always calling our names.) Recently, the Lord showed me a vision of what "awakened morning by morning" was like in the Garden of Eden. I saw Adam and Eve sleeping under a great tree until the sound of the Lord's footsteps awakened them. Adam opened his eyes and greeted the day while stretching his hands toward the sun. As the Lord approached, His smile cast a light upon them, even though it was already bright outside.

The Lord said, "Adam, Eve, come here. I want to show you something."

He then spent the day walking with them and explaining the creative process of the oceans and the purposes of each plant and tree. They walked together all day. Adam and Eve could ask any question they wanted to, and the Father would answer and explain profound mysteries in simple ways. When night came, Adam, Eve, and the Father sat on the edge of a vine-covered cliff, and the Father explained to them how He chose the location of each star for its specific purpose. That night, while Adam and Eve slept, they dreamed of the events of the day. The next morning, they were again awakened by the Lord as He came to walk with them and teach them of His creation and His character.

I believe that, in the Garden, they truly were awakened morning by morning by the Lord. This was God's original plan for His relationship with us. And it is still His longing today—that the first thought on our minds would be about Him. He still wants to walk with us along the streets of our lives—the smooth and the rocky alike—and teach us how to plant flowers in the midst of brokenness. He's inviting us, like my daughter Leila, to come along with Him. Many of His children have forgotten who they are and have run far from His arms, but He will never, ever give up on them. He wants to know, will we come along and walk the broken and dirty streets with Him? Will we help Him bring them home?

Faithful Friend

By Nic and Rachael Billman

I need You, Jesus
I don't know what to do without You, Jesus
What a faithful friend
What a faithful friend

In the season of brokenness
You plant seeds of restoration
In the soil of my repentance
And You water them with tears
And in my moments of unbelief
You just smile and say to me
I'm a faithful friend
I'm a faithful friend

Alleluia, alleluia, alleluia, alleluia

CHAPTER TWO

The Master's Touch

For it pleased the Father that in Him all the fullness should dwell, and by Him to reconcile all things to Himself, by Him, whether things on earth or things in heaven, having made peace through the blood of His cross.

—Colossians 1:19-20

I heard a story, once, of a live auction that had many of the usual items—antiques, paintings, and old tools. But the last item in the auction was an old, worn, and battered violin. The auctioneer started the bidding at one hundred dollars, but no one raised a hand.

"Eighty dollars," the auctioneer pleaded, but still, no one was interested.

Then, in the back of the room, an old, gray-haired man stood up; he walked to the front and picked up the old violin. After looking over the violin with a kind smile, he began to play a melody so beautiful the angels started to sing. The crowd sat in silent awe. After a few minutes, the old man stopped playing and gently put the violin down. As he walked back to his seat, a man with a black hat raised his hand and shouted, "One thousand dollars!"

"Fifteen hundred!" another man shouted from across the room.

"Two thousand!" shouted a woman on the front row.

"Twenty-five hundred!" responded the man with the black hat.

"Twenty-five hundred," said the auctioneer. "Going once, going twice, sold to the man in the black hat."

As the man and his son walked to their car, the son tugged on his

•father's coat and said, "I don't understand, Papa. No one was interested in the violin, even for one hundred dollars. But you just bought it for twenty-five hundred. What changed?"

With his treasured prize in hand, the man smiled and simply said, "The master's touch my boy, the master's touch."

More than Rescued

Like this violin, in the embrace of our Father, our true identities are revealed, and in His hands, our destinies are fulfilled. Some are worn and battered from the journey; others have been silenced by circumstances and trials. But in His hands, each one of us re-learns the music we were always meant to play. We come alive, because we are the song inside His heart.

The girls and boys whom we meet in rescue homes are beautiful examples of this. On my very first visit to one of these homes in Brazil, I was given a tour of the house and introduced to the thirteen girls who lived there, along with their house mom and dad. One girl in this home had been forced into prostitution at the age of nine so that her parents could afford to buy crack. Another girl was raped by her step-father at the age of fourteen and became pregnant; she now lives in the rescue home with her two-year-old daughter. One girl was repeatedly raped by both her mom and dad, along with their friends, from the age of twelve until she was rescued at age sixteen. Another girl was found, malnourished and nearly naked, searching for food in a dumpster and living homeless on the streets. I was overwhelmed and broken by their stories. I'm a father, and many of these girls were the same ages as my children.

After the tour, the house father asked if I would lead some worship on the porch. When I agreed, one of the girls brought me a guitar, and I began to strum and sing a simple love song to Jesus. As I sang, I looked up and saw all of these girls singing to Jesus with tears in their eyes and smiles on their faces. It was exactly how I picture the sinful woman looking as she washed Jesus's feet with her tears (see Luke 7:36-50). In that moment, I realized that those girls hadn't just been rescued; they'd been redeemed. They had lived lives worse than any nightmare I've ever had. They'd been abandoned, rejected, abused, betrayed, and sold by the very ones who were supposed to love and protect them. Yet despite these horrors, these girls *are* loved by their Father, and they *know* it!

This revelation of their value and identity as children of God has transformed them. They have found so much freedom and healing that, as their house father later told me, "these girls pray that their parents and abusers would experience the same freedom that they have." This is the core of redemption. They have prayed the prayer of Jesus, who—though He had been wrongfully accused, rejected, beaten, and crucified—looked down from the cross at the faces of His accusers and abusers and cried out, *"Father, forgive them, for they do not know what they do"* (Luke 23:34). Simply put, redemption gives us a new heart—our Father's heart—and we begin to see people the way He sees them. Like Him, we begin to long for the redemption of all things. We look with grace upon the accusers and abusers, upon the most offensive and destitute, and we invite them to join us and our Father. To come back home. As we walk the streets of this world with our Father, we see that His heart for all does not exclude anyone—not even the worst of abusers. Each one of us—if we are willing—will find our home in His heart.

Deep in Jesus's Heart

My children wrote a song about this several years ago. Being the children of musicians, they learned to play instruments at an early age. One night, when we were still living in Pennsylvania, the kids came bounding down the stairs and proudly announced, "It's time for the concert! Everybody come up stairs."

So Rachael and I went up to the kids' room, where they played several songs that they had written. All of the songs were special, but the last one wrecked me. The kids sang these words:

Deep in Jesus's heart, there is a place for you.
Deep in Jesus's heart there is a love for you.
And my name echoes in the chambers,
the chambers of His heart.

After clearing my throat, I said, "Wow, guys! Explain this song to me."

Christian said, "You know, Dad, it's in Jesus's heart where you hear your name."

So many people are asking, *Who am I? Where do I belong?* God has hidden the answer inside the heart of His Son. In His heart, we discover who we are and what we're worth to Him. As we are reunited with His heart, we find our song.

Redeemed for What?

In the Bible, this reunion with our Father is called redemption. As the girls at the rescue home illustrate, redemption is more than the great divine rescue mission. Yes, we are rescued, but the true value of the cross is found in what we are redeemed for. We're not just saved out of bad stuff, but we're saved into good stuff. Ephesians 1 gives us a great summary:

> *Blessed be the God and Father of our Lord Jesus Christ, who has blessed us with every spiritual blessing in the heavenly places in Christ, just as He chose us in Him before the foundation of the world, that we should be **holy** and **without blame** before Him **in love**, having predestined us to **adoption** as sons by Jesus Christ to himself, according to the good pleasure of His will* (Eph. 1:3-5).

This section of Ephesians 1 focuses on redemption, and in these three verses we find the four main purposes of redemption—holiness, blamelessness, love, and adoption. It also tells us that we were chosen *before* sin entered the world and humanity fell. When we put these together, we see that these four characteristics have been God's plan for us since before the world began. They are the underpinnings of His family. When sin got in the way, He sent Jesus to redeem us to holiness, blamelessness, love, and adoption so that we can rejoin the family as sons and daughters.

1. Holiness

First, He has redeemed us to holiness. Simply put, *holiness* means "to be like our Papa, Father God." The Lord tells us in First Peter 1:16, *"Be holy, for I am holy."* God is holy, and we are created in His image. Since the Fall of humanity, the only person to walk the earth in total holiness was Jesus. He lived a life of holiness, not only to die as a redemptive sacrifice for our sins, but also to give us a blueprint for how to live. Through His death on the cross, Jesus literally redeemed us into His holiness.

To understand what this means, we first need to look at the way things worked before Jesus came. Under the old covenant, only sanctified priests could enter the holy of holies, where the Arc of the Covenant and the presence of God resided. They could only enter because the proper sacrifices had been made. Ordinary people like us could not enter the holy of holies. In fact, sometimes even the chosen priest fell dead before the Lord.

However, when Jesus died on the cross, the curtain that separated the holy of holies from the other parts of the Temple was torn in two (see Matt. 27:51; Mark 15:38; Luke 23:45). The presence of God forever left the Arc and the holy of holies. Not long after, God established the new covenant when He found a new holy of holies to dwell in—His sons and daughters (see Acts 2). One day, there was a room where the presence of God dwelt, and we could not even enter that room. Then Jesus died on the cross and resurrected three days later—changing everything. Now, not only can we enter His presence, but we have become the room where He dwells—the place we once could not enter. We have become the dwelling place of the Holy Spirit.

Of course, God's plan was never for His presence to live in a box. But when humanity fell into sin, God needed to establish some boundaries. From that time forward, God anticipated the day when He could again live and walk with His children. We see His longing for it throughout the Old Testament, which is the story of His preparation and pursuit of His lost children for the moment of redemption—when they could again return to His side.

God's redemptive plan culminated in Jesus's death and resurrection, and because of His sacrifice, we can now stare into His eyes and behold His glory with unveiled faces. This causes us to transform into His image, which is exactly what redemption is all about (see 2 Cor. 3:18). He has restored us back to our original image by removing the separation between us and Him and allowing us to see Him face-to-face. Once again, we are at home.

2. Blamelessness

The second aspect of our redemption is blamelessness, which goes even deeper than sinlessness. If we are blameless, the accuser cannot even point to anything in our lives. There is no blame. Not only are we forgiven of our sins, but our sins are forgotten by the great King. When the accuser stands before God and attempts to bring accusations, he points his finger at us, but Jesus stands between us and the accuser. Jesus intercedes on our behalf, removing all blame, so that all the Father sees is Jesus in us. Blamelessness is the forgetfulness of God (see Ps. 103:10-12; Mic. 7:18-19).

Our sins are the only thing God ever forgets. Because of the sacrifice of Jesus, God forgets them, which means that we are not only forgiven, but we are without blame. We love to tell the women we meet who are living in prostitution that Jesus makes all things new. We tell them the story of Rahab, the prostitute, who has a place in the lineage of Jesus. He didn't come into the world through a pedigree of perfect people without fault; He came through a bloodline of imperfect people, and by His blood, all things are made new and all blame is removed.

3. Love

Third, we are redeemed for love. The phrase *"before Him in love"* refers to abiding in God's love. God has always loved all of His children, even when we have been far from Him. His love is nonnegotiable. At the same time, He doesn't want that love to be one-way. He wants us to walk with Him and to abide in His love, just like Adam and Eve did in the Garden of Eden. He longs for intimacy with His children.

When Jesus came, He preached the Father's heart, saying things like, "Abide in Me and I will abide in you" (see John 15:4) and, "The Son can do nothing apart from the Father" (see John 5:19). Through His life, Jesus restored the example of a child abiding in the love of the Father, and through His death and resurrection, He sealed the deal so that we can abide in His love forever.

One time, while I was preaching, I saw a quick vision of Jesus after the resurrection. He went in the spirit to the angel who had been assigned to guard the entrance of Eden, He put His arm around the angel, and He said, "Hey man, you've done a good job, but your shift is up. You can take your sword and get back to worship in Heaven. God's people can abide with Him in paradise once again." Jesus restored us to a life of habitation in God's love.

4. Adoption

The fourth aspect of redemption is our adoption into God's family. In the beginning, as we already discussed, life in the Garden was about fellowship between the Father and His children. Ever since the Fall, God's ultimate plan has been to get His kids back. The cross was not just a reaction to sin and satan; it was the signature on the adoption paperwork, signed with the blood of Jesus. Though the Father chose us before sin existed, because of the burden of sin, He had to pay the price to bring us home.

My little brother was adopted by my parents, and I always tell him, "Mom and Dad didn't have a choice with me, but they chose you!" It's a joke, but it's true. To be adopted means that we were chosen, and a price was paid to make us sons and daughters. It also means that we share in the inheritance of our parents just like a biological child. As children of God, we share in the inheritance of the Father just as Jesus does. Romans 8:15-17 sums this up beautifully:

> For you did not receive the spirit of bondage again to fear, but you received the Spirit of adoption by whom we cry out, "Abba, Father." The Spirit Himself bears witness with our spirit that we are children of God, and if children, then heirs—heirs of God and joint heirs with Christ, if indeed we suffer with Him, that we may also be glorified together.

Jesus is the only person recorded in the Bible who prayed, "Abba Father"—in His prayer in the Garden of Gethsemane before the crucifixion (see Mark 14:36). *Abba* is an intimate Hebrew word for "father." It could be translated into English as "daddy." This prayer is unique because it would be like saying, "Daddy Father." My friend, Adam LiVecchi, suggests that Jesus prayed that way in one of His greatest moments of weakness because He had a child's heart of dependence as well as the heart of a mature Son.

The full prayer went like this: *"Abba, Father, all things are possible for You. Take this cup away from Me; nevertheless, not what I will, but what You will."* The first part portrays the heart of a child: "Daddy, this task before me is too much for me to bear." It shows His dependence on and need of Daddy. The second part is the voice of the mature Son: "Not my will, but yours be done." Jesus understood the balance of the two. We are to be, like children, totally dependent upon Papa, but we are also called to be mature sons and daughters who will always choose the will of the Father over our own desires.

Paul quotes the phrase that Jesus prayed twice, once in Romans 8 (above) and again in Galatians 4:6: *"And because you are sons, God has sent forth the Spirit of His Son into your hearts, crying out, 'Abba, Father!'"* Paul understood this balance because he lived in a time when he could trust few and was totally dependent upon the Father, yet he willingly paid a great price to bear the cup that was handed to him. Paul's message is both simple and profound. Because we are sons and daughters, God has given us the spirit of His Son so that we too can pray the prayer of Jesus—"Abba Father." Everywhere we go, I tell people that the most powerful prayer you can pray is, "Abba Father," or, "Come Papa," because when our Daddy comes, hearts and atmospheres change.

All for Us

In these four aspects of redemption, we see that God did not send His only Son to die for our sins just so that we could be forgiven and one day go to Heaven. He sent Jesus so that we could be redeemed and have abundant life here on earth. Forgiveness is a part of redemption, but it's just a part. God removed our sins with a purpose—so that He could fill the space that was formerly occupied by sin and death with His Spirit. He removed our sins because sin distorts our view of our identity, and He wanted to reestablish *sonship* in our hearts. Simply put, *sonship* is a lifestyle rooted in our identity as sons and daughters of the Father. Everything we say and do flows from our understanding of who we are as His kids.

Redemption isn't just about Jesus's death on the cross but about the life that He lived, walking as a true Son with the Father. He modeled sonship for us. Then He redeemed us from sin and death, not just so that we can go to Heaven, but so that we can live as adopted sons and daughters on this earth. The goal of redemption is that we would walk with Him, confident in our identity as His children, and learn to follow His lead (see John 5:19), to become just like our Daddy.

Just Like Daddy

Children naturally imitate their fathers. Even from birth, babies learn facial reactions and emotions by watching their parents' faces. I love making faces at my baby daughter, Cássia, and watching her mimic my face right back to me. Just as children imitate their fathers from a young age, we are to imitate Father God. As Ephesians 5:1-2 says,

> *Therefore be imitators of God as dear children. And walk in love, as Christ also has loved us and given Himself for us, an offering and a sacrifice to God for a sweet-smelling aroma.*

We imitate Him by walking in love just like Jesus and by living our lives as sweet-smelling sacrifices to God. When we look at the life of Jesus, we will know how to imitate the Father to our generation.

My daughter Leila, in her simplicity as a child, illustrates well what it means to follow our Father's lead. Once, when she was three years old, she accompanied me to the weekly worship and prayer service at the church we were, at that time, pastoring in Texas. That night, a visiting woman came with one of our church members. She was in her early forties and was very sad. Several of our people attempted to comfort her and pray with her, but she didn't respond. We had a worship CD playing, and Leila had been dancing, as little girls do. I watched her as she locked eyes on our sad visitor. She was reading her emotions and felt compassion for her. Leila walked over and sat next to the woman. She tapped her shoulder and said, "I know your mommy left you, but your Daddy will never leave you."

At that, the woman burst into tears and began sobbing. Leila just smiled and skipped off to her next adventure. Through Leila's words, the wall around this woman's heart came down, and as she cried, one of our ministry team members was able to counsel her and love on her. The woman explained that her mother had abandoned her when she was little; as a result, she had always had issues trusting people and especially God. Leila's word of knowledge was like a key that unlocked all of that pain and brokenness and ushered in freedom. Seeing the sad woman, Leila simply listened to her Father and delivered His message.

Leila also likes to play a game called "Where's Jesus." It's basically hide-and-seek with Jesus. When we're leading worship or ministering to people, she likes to look around the room and see where she sees Jesus. If she sees Jesus hugging someone, she goes and hugs that person. If she sees Jesus praying for someone, she goes and prays for that person. If she sees Jesus dancing, she'll go and dance. If she sees Jesus lying on the floor in worship, she'll lie down and do the same.

One night we were at a great church in the Chicago area, and God dropped an absolute love bomb on us. In the aftermath, people were sitting and lying all over the place, and Leila was looking for Jesus. One lady was sitting on the ground, and Leila came over and said, "You should move. There is an angel praying for that lady standing next to you, and she's about to fall on you."

The lady, who told us this story later that night, said she obliged Leila because she thought she was cute. But as soon as she moved, the woman standing next to her fell exactly where she had been sitting. No one was praying for the woman, but Leila had seen the angel in the spirit and gave our new friend a heads-up! As soon as the woman fell, the lady Leila had spoken to said, "Leila, pray for me!"

Walking with Jesus and ministering to others really is as simple as playing hide-and-seek with Jesus. It's looking for Jesus and then doing the things that He does; in other words, it's living in sonship. This is what we've been redeemed for.

Delight

By Nic and Rachael Billman

I delight in you, I delight in you
I delight in you, I delight in you
Every step that you take brings a smile to my face
Every step that you take brings a smile to my face

And You get down on Your knees
And look through the open skies
And you say, "Gather around call the angels
Call everyone in town
Just wait and see, just wait and see
What my daughter will do"

Cause you're not watching with anticipation
For failure
You are watching with expectation of my victory
And when I fall down it's the sound of your laugh
That brings me back to my feet

CHAPTER THREE

The Father's Delight

He also brought me out into a broad place;
He delivered me because He delighted in me.

—Psalm 18:19

⟋⟋⟋

ecently, while I was sitting in our living room, my youngest daughter, Cássia, crawled in and decided that she was going to attempt to take her first steps. I called Rachael and the other kids, and we all watched with smiles on our faces saying, "She's going to do it! Watch! She's going to walk!" Over and over, she tried to take a step, fell down, and then cried. She felt frustrated, but I wasn't worried or saddened by her struggle. Instead, I laughed because I delight in her every move. Each time she fell, I said, "It's okay, baby. You can do it." Hearing my voice, she'd look up, see my smile, hear my laugh, and decide to try once more. Again, we would all watch with such excitement and joy.

Our Father God watches us like this, continually delighting in us. He gathers all of Heaven and says, "Just watch what my son will do! Just wait and see the next step my daughter will take!" Even when we fall, He is such a compassionate Father that He just picks us up and says, "It's okay. Let's try again." Like a good father, He doesn't see us according to our deficiencies but through the eyes of destiny and love.

Not long after Cássia's attempt at walking, I spent some time worshipping with our ministry staff in Brazil. Over and over, I sang a simple phrase to the Lord—"I delight in You."

After a while, I heard Him singing over me, "I delight in you," and then I saw a vision of God in Heaven. He was lying on His belly, looking through a great hole in the heavens, and He was watching us. He was pointing His finger at each one of us, but He wasn't pointing with disappointment or with expectation for failure. He had a big smile on His face, and He called out to the heavens, "Everyone gather around, call the angels, call everyone in town. Just wait and see what my son will do next."

Somehow the phrase, "God is watching us" has picked up a negative connotation. But God isn't sitting up in Heaven watching over us to make sure that we don't fail. In the same way that I watched Cássia attempt to walk, God is watching us with joy and expectation for our victory. And He delights in our every move along the way. Even when we fall, His delight in us is unswerving.

"I Love Your Song"

In fact, the Bible tells us that the Father sings over us with great joy:

> The Lord your God in your midst, the Mighty One, will save; He will rejoice over you with gladness, He will quiet you with His love, He will rejoice over you with singing (Zeph. 3:17).

This song the Father sings is not just for the children who have already come home. It's for all of His children. In fact, it starts with a declaration of His power to save, showing us the way He aims His joy, gladness, and love toward the lost. He delights in them, not because of their circumstances, because they are beautiful to Him. He knows what they are made for, and He sings out His joyful expectation of their discovery of themselves in His love.

When I am on the streets (or anywhere, really), I like to listen for what the Father is singing over people, and then I sing it to them. Recently, we were on the streets of Recife in a section of town that is notorious for prostitution. It's a five-kilometer stretch of road about one block from the beach. On any given night, four or five girls are standing on every corner. On this night, we were handing out roses and The Father's Love Letter[1] to the girls. We gave each one a rose and told them how beautiful they are to the Father and that we had a love letter from Him for them. After an hour, we ran out of roses and love letters, but continued on, equipped only with the love of God. His love is always enough!

As we approached one group of girls, I heard the Lord singing over one of them, and I saw a quick vision of her holding a microphone. He was singing, "I love your song. I love your song."

I asked her, "Do you like to sing?" She sheepishly admitted that she did. I told her, "When I saw you, I saw a vision of you holding a microphone, and I heard Father God singing over you, 'I love your song.' I want to tell you that He loves your song; He loves to hear you sing. Even when you're all alone in the shower and you think no one hears you, He hears you, and He loves your song."

She began to cry and shared with us that she was eighteen years old, a mother of two, and had only been prostituting for three months to pay the bills. She tearfully told us that she had been taking singing lessons and that she hopes that one day she will be able to support her daughters by using her voice instead of her body. We prayed for her and took her phone number so we could continue the relationship.

The Simple Gospel

The gospel is really as simple as this picture of the Father singing over us with joy as we learn to walk. It's not easy, but it is simple. Walking the streets of Brazil and taking the love of the Father to the lost forces us to keep the gospel simple. We have to describe it in a way that they will receive. We don't water it down; we just stick to the point. We paint an image of the compassionate Father who wants His kids back. We tell them about the delighted Father who believes in and celebrates each of His children, even when they fall down. Too often in the Church, we make the mistake of trying to answer questions the world is not asking. This only leads to arguments, frustration, and confusion. Our Papa is a great listener; He hears our prayers and the cries of our hearts. When we talk to people, we try to be like Him and listen to their heart cry—which is always for identity and value.

With this as our motto, we can describe the gospel to an alcoholic homeless man—who has seemingly drunk his life away—by telling him that God is a loving Father who wants His kids back and has paid the price to get them. We can say something like, "You are His son, and He values you so much that He gave His Son to die on the cross so that He could get you back" (see John 3:16). Chances are, the drunk won't fall to his knees, repent, and accept Jesus immediately. Sometimes that happens, but certainly not most of the time. We're not too concerned about that, though, because we've started a relationship with this man by declaring to him how God—and we—value him.

The two most important bridges that we build for the lost are identity and value. The lost have a poor concept of true value, basing everything upon a monetary system. Similarly, they base identity on what a person does and who a person knows. This is the crisis before us. A large number of people don't know who they are and don't realize their true value. This is true in all facets of society, but it is especially true when ministering to people in prostitution. Their idea of value, in a very personal way, has been reduced to "How much are you willing to pay for my services?"

One night, we were on the streets ministering to a group of prostitutes. One of our team members, Jonathan, was talking to a girl named Natalie. Natalie is about twenty-two years old, and she has been in prostitution since she was sixteen. As Jonathan was talking to her, a man came over and pointed to a group of drunk teenage boys across the street. He said, "Those boys want to pay you fifty reais to go to a motel and have sex with them." She responded and told him that her rate was eighty reais. As the man went to deliver the new price to the boys, Jonathan pleaded with her not to take the job for fear of her safety.

Then she turned to him and said, "Can you believe that they thought that I was worth fifty reais? I am worth eighty reais."

Jonathan told her, "You are worth so much more than eighty reais or any amount of money." Thankfully, she ended up not taking the job that night, and we had a chance, over time, to build a relationship with her. Yet her words to Jonathan, "I am worth eighty reais," reveal the heartbreaking reality of the world's value system. In response, the Father is crying out,

"You are worth so much more than that! You have no idea how much I paid for your freedom!" This is the gospel. We deliver the cry of the Father's heart to the lost. We tell them that they are His sons and daughters. We tell them how valuable they are to Him and the price that He has paid for them. We tell them that He finds great delight in them.

It's a simple gospel. Once the questions of value and identity are settled, the other questions that people have can be answered along the way, as they get to know the Father. If we begin to answer those questions before we have told them about their identity and value, it leads us down a dangerous pathway. Too many Christians have received Jesus because it "made sense," but years later, they are still asking, *Who am I?* As we discussed in the last chapter, we discover our true identity as we learn to know Father God.

What Fathers Do

Children learn who they are by interacting with their parents. When I rejoiced over Cassia's efforts to walk, I wasn't just encouraging her toward success. I was actually imparting identity and value to her. I was saying, "You're worth so much to me that I'm okay with your process. Even if you don't get it right this time, my love for you and your status as my child won't change." This is what fathers do. They tell their children who they are. Mothers do this, too, of course, but fathers have a unique role in speaking identity and destiny into the lives of their children. The encouragement of a father instills identity inside a child and establishes a foundation for the child's destiny. Thus, the success of our destiny is directly related to the foundation our identity is built upon.

Unfortunately, in our generation, divorce, broken homes, and fatherlessness are rampant. Many people grow up with fathers who fail to impart positive identity or value to them; others grow up with no father at all. In Brazil, for example, approximately fifty percent of homes do not have fathers, and one-third of the children do not even have a father's name on their birth certificates. It's not surprising, then, that we have a generation that is crying out, *Who am I?* The real problem isn't drugs, prostitution, violence, or crime; those are all by-products of the real problem— fatherlessness. And the real answer is a revelation of the delighted Father and the value and identity He instills in us as He encourages us toward our destiny in Him. As sons and daughters of the Father, we are called to join Him in speaking identity and destiny into the people of our generation. We are called to reflect the voice and heart of a Father who takes great delight in them.

Recently, we were on the streets of Natal, a city notorious for child prostitution in Northeast Brazil. There, we talked with two teenage transvestites, Jonathan, sixteen, and Ariel, seventeen. They were very open with us, and Jonathan shared that his father was an Assemblies of God pastor. He had started prostituting when he was thirteen as a boy and slowly transformed himself to look like a girl. His father then kicked him out of his house and forbid him from coming back to the church because he said he was an embarrassment to him. Now he is sixteen, and he recently tried to return home to his parents, but his father violently threw him out the door and onto the street. Jonathan's elbows were still cut and bruised from this rejection, but the pain in his heart was much deeper.

Ariel also started prostituting when he was very young; he couldn't even remember how old he was when he began. They both told us that most of their clients are married men, many of them Christians who sneak away from their homes; some of them are even pastors. We hear this often on the streets of Brazil. Ariel said he attended church as a child, but people there would either make fun of him or tell him he was going to hell. As a young child, perhaps ten years old, he was struggling with his identity and prostituting for older men on the streets—and at church, people made fun of him. It's no wonder these boys have a negative image of God and His family! They see a Father who rejects and abuses them and a family that makes fun of them, ignoring their cries for help. Through it all, the great question echoed in their hearts: *Who am I?*

They needed to see the Father as He really is and to hear the words of value and identity He speaks to them. Unfortunately, the very people who should have been conveying the message had done just the opposite. I said to these boys, "I am a Christian and a member of the Church. Would you please forgive me on behalf of the Church for the way that you were treated?"

They were speechless. Then Ariel said, with tears in his eyes, "I know that what I'm doing is wrong. I know deep down inside that this is not who I am. But why did the devil choose me to torment? Why didn't he choose you? What did I do to deserve this?"

I put my arm around him and told him, "The devil torments all of us in different ways. The reason he chose you is because he knows something that you don't. He knows how special you are and the destiny that God has for you, and that makes him afraid, so he will try to steal, kill, and destroy that destiny. But I'm here to tell you how special you really are to the Father. He loves you and is longing for you to return to His arms so you can discover that destiny together."

It's not complicated. When people reveal to us the lies that they've been living in, we reveal to them the truth of the gospel. We tell them who they are and where they belong, and we invite them to return to their Father's arms and experience the way He delights in them. He is such a good Father.

A Beautiful Gift

One time, while we were leading worship at one of our ministry schools in Brazil, the Lord took me into an open vision. What I saw perfectly describes the heart of our Father and the delight He takes in each one of His children. In the vision, I saw worship in Heaven as described in Revelation 4. I saw the Abba King sitting on the throne, and the angels and the four living creatures were surrounding the throne in worship.

I watched as the twenty-four elders entered the throne room with their crowns upon their heads. As they bowed before the throne, they cast their crowns to the ground before the King, and I heard the sound of the crowns, like metal hitting the floor. The crowns that we bring before the Lord are our honor, our successes, our victories, our ministries, and all of the good things that we have for an offering. In my vision, every time an elder would cast his crown down in surrender, the Abba King would smile from the throne and say, "Thank you! What a beautiful gift you've brought Me."

After the elders finished, they joined the angels in worship, and I saw a new group of people enter the throne room. The broken came, dragging their chains behind them as they approached the throne. One by one, they threw their chains down before the King, and it sounded like metal hitting the floor. The chains represent our sins, struggles, and failures. Every time one of these broken ones threw the chains to the ground, the Abba King would smile and say, "Thank you! What a beautiful gift you've brought Me."

Our King is a God who takes the trophies of saints and the garments of sinners, and He calls them the same. It's not so much what we bring before the King but how we bring it. Jesus made this clear when He spoke of people who do all kinds of wonderful things in His name but didn't actually *know* Him; in the end, He will tell them to depart from His presence (see Matt. 7). In contrast, so many people have come to Jesus with nothing to give Him but their sins and a broken heart, and He has made them "fishers of men." People all too often judge by appearances, but God sees us by our hearts. When we come home to our Father, He receives us and delights in us. It is that simple.

We see no better reflection of this than in the nativity story (see Luke 2; Matt. 1–2). Jesus, the King of kings and Lord of lords, was born in the lowliest of places. At His birth, the poor and the rich came to worship. The shepherds came with nothing to offer but their worship and honor. The three wise men came with their royal gifts of gold, frankincense, and myrrh. Both forms of offering were received and accepted as worship before the King. This is the Abba King we worship—who receives our gifts with love and grace, even when our hands our empty.

Let the Children Come

Whenever I think about the vision that I had of worship in Heaven, I think about the many men and women in prostitution we've met on the streets of Brazil. One time, Rachael and I were having dinner with Rosana, a friend of ours whom we first met on the streets in 2009. She has been in prostitution for over twenty years. As we talked with her about how valuable she is to the Father and the price that He paid for her, she began to cry. She said, "He did all of that for me, and I have nothing to give back to Him. He wasted it."

We told her, "That's right. He wasted it all and didn't even hold back one drop because He knew you were worth it. The only thing that He wants is your heart. He paid the price to give you an offering worthy of a king: your heart."

At that she cried and simply said, "How can He be so good?"

In the world's eyes (sometimes we in the Church see with the world's eyes), these people have nothing to give, no offering to bring. They're like the children who were brought to Jesus in Mark 10. The disciples couldn't see their value and only saw them as an annoyance. Yet Jesus rebuked the disciples, saying, *"Let the little children come to Me, and do not forbid them; for of such is the Kingdom of God"* (Mark 10:14).

The lost sons and daughters on the streets of Brazil are simply children who have faced hindrances in knowing Jesus. It may seem like they have little or nothing to offer, but Jesus's arms are open, and He's saying, *"Let the children come to me..."* The passage tells us about two types of people—those who tried to send the children away and those who brought the children to Jesus so that He might bless them. God is earnestly seeking people in our generation, in all nations, who will seek and find the children and bring them home to the Father so that they might experience His delight and live in His blessing.

Shores of Grace

By Nic and Rachael Billman

You are the father to the fatherless
The mother to the orphan child
You are the open arms to the prodigal
The grace for the harlot daughter
There is nothing apart from Your love

You are the kiss upon the widow's lips
Life inside the barren womb
You are the vision in the eyes of the blind
The song in the ears of the deaf
There is nothing apart from Your love

And my heart is broken on the shores of Your grace
And my soul is overwhelmed in the ocean of Your love
Show me how to love so I can love with Your heart
Teach me how to see so I can see with Your eyes

You dance in the paintings of the blind
You dwell in the melodies of the mute
You're revealed in the suffering of the sick
You rejoice in the fellowship of the poor
Show us how to love

CHAPTER FOUR

The Compassionate Father

But when he was still a great way off, his father
saw him and had compassion, and ran and fell
on his neck and kissed him.

—Luke 15:20

~~~~~~~~ ⟟ ⟟ ~~~~~~~~

In November of 1985, my cousin, Jimmy, visited his parents in Pennsylvania. Jimmy was living in Chicago at the time with his wife and baby daughter. He was twenty-six years old, good-looking, and strong, weighing about 190 pounds. He was enjoying his life with his family and seemed to be in good health, with the exception of some complaints about a few aches and pains.

Seven months later, in June of 1986, Jimmy lay in a hospital bed, weighing about eighty pounds. Gaunt and covered in sores, he was dying of complications due to AIDS. The nurse wore a mask and rubber gloves as she gave my uncle an update on Jimmy's status, and she advised that my aunt and uncle also wear a mask and gloves if they wanted to have contact with him. In 1986, people lived in great fear of AIDS and HIV, and some believed one could catch the disease simply through germs in breath or in saliva. In that era, as far as people understood, the nurse had good reason to suggest a mask and gloves.

As she said these words to my uncle, he looked at his son; he saw his open, oozing sores, his chest lumbering for each breath, and his sunken and pale face. He looked at the nurse and said, "This is my son, and I love him. I don't need a mask and gloves." He wanted his son to feel his father's touch on his skin, he wanted him to see his father face-to-face, and he wanted him to hear his voice clearly. My aunt and uncle went into the room where Jimmy lay and, as hard as it was, they cherished those last moments with their son. Jimmy died as my aunt and uncle sat on the bed holding his hands and singing, "Jesus Loves Me" to him. A few months earlier, my grandfather had gone to visit Jimmy and had prayed with him to give his heart to Jesus. Despite the agony of losing him, my family was blessed to know that he ran into the open arms of Jesus that day. When he died, he entered into no more pain, no more sickness, and no more death—only life.

A Mask and Gloves

Through this whole process, the Lord began to speak to my uncle. He said, "Jim, just as you didn't wear a mask and gloves to embrace your son, I didn't wear a mask and gloves when I embraced the world. I came in the flesh, and I embraced you in your sin and sickness, with your open sores and wounds. In fact, I took on your sin and sickness so that you could feel My embrace and know My love."

Many people view God as an angry God who sits in Heaven and throws lightning bolts if we step out of His will. Somewhere along the way, many of us started believing that God hates the world. But as we discussed in the last chapter, that is the antithesis of the gospel; John 3:16 tells the truth. God looked upon the world, wallowing in sin and sickness, and His heart was so moved by compassion that He paid the ultimate price, giving His only Son so that we could have everlasting life with Him. It's true that sin and sickness sadden the heart of God, but His love is not contingent upon us living sin-free and healthy lives. He delights in us for who we are—who He created us to be. And as a compassionate Father, He sent Jesus to not only cure our sin and sickness, but to *become* our sin and sickness so that He could overcome them forever on the cross.

My uncle is often asked, "How did Jimmy get AIDS?"

His response has always been, "I don't know. I never asked." To him, it didn't matter how his son got sick; it only mattered that he knew that his father wasn't going to abandon him.

I've always admired my uncle for that. It reminds me of the father in the story of the lost son in Luke 15. When the son returned to his father, he wasn't greeted with, "Where have you been, young man?" In fact, according to the story, the son was sitting in the pigpen when he decided to return home and offer his services as a hired worker. Pigpens house a limited number of items—pigs, mud, rotten food, and of course, pig crap. The story says nothing about the son pausing to take a shower or wash up, but it does say he was greeted with his father's embrace. Even when we're covered in crap, God embraces us. *He* cleanses us and puts a robe on our backs and a ring on our fingers.

To get a better understanding of the compassionate heart of the Father, let's take a closer look at that story.

Our True Inheritance

In the parable, we read about a man who had two sons, the younger of which asked his father for his inheritance. In that culture, a son was not to request his inheritance; this was an extreme dishonor. A son only received his inheritance when he married or when the father died. The younger son was essentially saying, "Father, you're dead to me, so give me my money." As requested, the father divided up the inheritance and gave the appropriate portion to each son. Promptly, the younger son gathered up his inheritance and left for a far off country, where he wasted it in reckless living. Jesus leaves out the details of *how* the son spent his money, simply calling it "reckless living." To Jesus, it's not important how we wasted our inheritance; all He cares about is restoring us to the arms of the Father.

After the son exhausted his inheritance, we find him sitting in the pigpen, envious of the pigs because they are filling themselves with old corncobs and scraps of rotten food. His envy of the pigs can mean only one thing; he was in a very bad place. Confronted by the mess he had created, his heart began to change. He thought to himself, *Even the hired servants in my father's house have enough bread to spare, but I'm sitting here hungry.* So he came up with a plan.

I will arise and go to my father, and will say to him, "Father, I have sinned against heaven and before you, and I am no longer worthy to be called your son. Make me like one of your hired servants" (Luke 15:18).

He didn't think to himself, *Man, I wish I had more money so I could go back to living large.* Often, we say we want restoration, but we really want better conditions or second chances. The son did not fall into that trap. His desire for restoration was real, and his heart began to long for the house of his father. As this story shows us, the journey to restoration begins when our longing for the Father is stronger than our desire for false satisfaction and temporary pleasures. Consumed with a desire for home, the son started on his long journey back down the road. The same road that had once led him to his destruction now led him back to the arms of his father.

Now for the best part! While the son was still a long way off, the father saw him and ran to him. This was a very counter-cultural move. Jewish law said that if a child was rebellious, he could be taken before the elders and stoned to death (see Deut. 21:18-21). But in Jesus's story, the father ran to be the first to meet his son so that there would be no question of punishment. The Jewish people listening to this story would have expected the son to be disciplined or even stoned, but suddenly they were hearing a new perspective. In the Jewish customs of that day, fathers also did not run toward their children. Fathers commanded great honor and respect, and they expected their children to come to them. By contrast, the father in this story demonstrates Father God's lavish love when a lost son returns home. Rather than waiting for us to get to Him, He runs toward us, longing to welcome us home.

As father and son embraced, the son knew what he must say: *"Father, I have sinned against heaven and in your sight, and am no longer worthy to be called your son"* (Luke 15:21). That's all he was able to get out, because his father didn't let him finish. He shouted out to his servants, "Bring the best robe in the house, bring a ring for his finger, and bring sandals for his feet," and then he threw him the greatest party the land had ever seen (see Luke 15:22-24).

The symbolism in the father's gifts to his son show us some very important aspects of the Father's compassion. The robe represents righteousness. When he gave him his robe, the father declared the son was forgiven and blameless in his sight. The son had sinned against the father; now the father demanded that all must see the boy through his eyes. The sandals represent two things. First, they indicate a cleansing from the journey. The father placing new shoes upon the son's dusty and dirty feet mirrors Jesus's washing of the disciples' feet. Second, the sandals also represent freedom. In those days, slaves did not typically wear shoes because they were not free to come and go as they pleased. However, sons and bondservants wore shoes because, although they served the master, they had freedom to go. Finally, the ring represents authority and inheritance.

The son had wasted every last penny of what was given to him, but his true inheritance was never in money, gold, or possessions. The true inheritance of sons and daughters is found in the heart of the Father. The son had been living in his inheritance his whole life in the house of his father. This is the best inheritance for a child—living within the house of the father and abiding in his love. This is far greater than receiving the wealth of the father through death or separation. Our God is a wealthy King, and He owns the cattle on a thousand hills, but our true inheritance is found within His heart. As Jesus put it in John 17:3, *"This is eternal life, that they may* [intimately] *know You, the only true God, and Jesus Christ whom You have sent."* The joy of being a child of God is found in spending an eternity discovering the hidden treasure within the heart of our Father! This has been His plan for us from the beginning, and this is what His compassion is winning us back for.

The Older Son Syndrome

Unfortunately, not everyone is willing to accept this image of the Father. Not everyone appreciates the compassion that fuels His actions. In Jesus's story, the older son was angered by his father's compassion for his brother. *"But he was angry and would not go in. Therefore his father came out and pleaded with him"* (Luke 15:28).

At the beginning of this story, in verse twelve, it says that the Father divided his wealth' and gave the appropriate portion to each son. In other words, the older son had already received his inheritance, too. Yet when he saw the joy of his father upon his brother's return, jealousy began to brew in his heart. He stayed out in the fields working, refusing to join in the festivities. When the father found him, the older son said,

> *These many years I have been serving you; I never transgressed your commandment at any time; and yet you never gave me a young goat, that I might make merry with my friends. But as soon as this son of yours came, who has devoured your livelihood with harlots, you killed the fatted calf for him* (Luke 15:29-30).

The older son referred to his brother as *"this son of yours,"* refusing to even claim him as his brother. And he had no compunctions about specifically naming his brother's sins. He was quick to point the finger of accusation and to bemoan his own situation. Though the older son had stayed within the father's house, he still didn't recognize his inheritance. Although the lifestyles and actions of the two brothers were very different, their mistake was the same. Neither one of them recognized that their true inheritance was their father's love and the opportunity to abide in that love. The fields of the older son can keep people just as far from their inheritance as the pigpen of the younger son.

The compassionate father loved both of his sons. He ran to meet the younger son on the road as he returned from his rebellion. And he left the party to find the older son working in the fields. The younger son recognized the goodness of his father while he was still in the pigpen. The older son failed to recognize the father's goodness, even when he was standing in his presence. The Father will always seek and find us; whether or not we will recognize Him and receive His compassion is determined by the attitude of our hearts. If we are willing, we will see that our inheritance lies in relationships with our Father, in the invitation to walk with Him through this life.

The Abundant Life

Another image that the Bible often uses to describe the invitation to restored relationship with our Father is the banquet table. In the Jewish culture, meals were covenantal. They shared life around the table; they laughed and cried together while sharing a meal. They talked about God and religion, and they talked about fishing and taxes. They talked about weddings and babies, and they talked about harvest and planting. Even the manner in which they sat was intimate. Most tables were low to the ground, and people sat on cushions or even reclined on each other. It was a time of communion together.

The definition of *communion* is the sharing or exchanging of intimate thoughts or feelings, especially when the exchange is on a mental or spiritual level. Ultimately, *communion* is the exchange of intimate thoughts and feelings with Jesus. It's exchanging our ashes for beauty and our brokenness for wholeness. It's sharing our thankfulness for all that He has done. With this in mind, we love to rent private rooms at fancy restaurants and have banquets for women on the streets. When we do, we bring a tangible revelation of the Father's table and His love for them. It is amazing to watch their faces as they are loved and honored, sitting at the table with Papa God.

The Jewish culture described intimacy of relationship and communion with this phrase—*This is the abundant life!* In that context, Jesus declared that He came to give us the abundant life (see John 10:10). Often, we think of *abundance* in terms of prosperity and provision, but the expression is actually rooted in relationship. As Jews sat around the table, they would take the bread and break it, and as they passed the broken bread to their neighbor, they would say, "This is the abundant life." In other words, they were saying, "This relationship and this togetherness is the abundant life." The actions of Jesus at the last supper were not uncommon to their culture. It was normal to break bread and pass the wine. What Jesus did differently on that night was say, "This is My body broken for you," and "This is My blood poured out for you" (see Luke 22:19-20). He became the covenant that guaranteed us a spot at the table of abundant life.

When Jesus said, *"The thief does not come except to steal, and to kill, and to destroy. I have come that they may have life, and that they may have it more abundantly"* (John 10:10), He was saying, "I have come to live and walk with you through this life together." He was promising, "I will never leave you nor forsake you. On the heights of the mountains and in the depths of the valleys, I will always walk with you." The abundant life *is* life with Jesus. He is the abundance. As my friend, Kevin Prosch, says, "The giver became the gift."[1]

Behavior vs. Identity

The abundant life was the true inheritance in Jesus's story of the two sons, and it is ours as well. But our ability to accept it is connected to our way of living, as the term *prodigal son* demonstrates. We think as either a prodigal or a son; we view ourselves based on our behavior or our identity. Of course, the father never referred to his son as "my prodigal son"; rather, it is a term added by Bible translators to describe the boy's behavior. It means "to be reckless, wasteful, or out of control."[2] To the Father, our value is not determined by our behavior, but by our identity. The boy's identity wasn't in his wasteful and reckless behavior, but in his position as a son to the father.

This issue of behavior versus identity is so important, because the devil wants to turn our behavior into a label. He takes the things we've done and tries to make them our identity. For example, if a person has a problem with drinking, that person may say, "I am an alcoholic." Or the person who has a problem with lying may say, "I am a liar." I'm not suggesting that we shouldn't recognize our sins or our struggles, but I am saying that, as we do, we must remember *who we are!* The devil doesn't just want us to act sinfully; he wants sin to become our identity. As Jesus said, the devil wants to steal, kill, and destroy (see John 10:10). The devil will always refer to us by our behavior, but the Father will always refer to us by our identity.

My brother, Luke, battled drug addiction for many years. One time, after returning home from prison, he came into the kitchen with his shirt off. My dad, who was sitting at the table, looked up to see a large pentagram tattoo on Luke's back. He then audibly heard the devil say to him, "See, I've marked your boy."

But then he audibly heard God say, "But I marked him first."

My dad clung to that hope throughout Luke's struggle with drugs and crime. One time, Luke had been missing on the streets for several months— no phone call, no news, nothing. Finally, one day he called from jail; he had been arrested for possession of drugs and robbery. As my brother tells the story, he was waiting in the visiting area, and when he first saw my dad walk in, he was so ashamed and embarrassed. My dad took Luke in his arms and said, "You are my son. I love you, and nothing will change that." Luke had to hide his face from the other prisoners as he wept on my dad's chest for about twenty minutes.

That wasn't the last time that Luke went missing or that my dad had to see him in jail. Many of my dad's days off and much of his vacation time during those years was used for visits to jail, rehabilitation centers, or far away correctional facilities. At one point, when we hadn't heard from Luke in months, my dad was in Toronto at a pastor's conference. During the conference, he had a vision of Luke preaching with his hand extended as he declared the gospel. My dad made a decision that day that he would keep that as his vision of his son rather than the drugs, crime, and violence or the nightmares and fear that the enemy used to torment. He chose to hold on to that vision of Luke's true identity in the eyes of the Father, despite his circumstances or behavior.

Finally, after about ten years, Luke overcame his drug addiction. He was attending Narcotics Anonymous meetings at the time, and one day he told me, "I don't think I'm going to go anymore." When I asked him why, he said, "Because I'm tired of claiming every week 'My name is Luke, and I'm an addict.' That's not who I am anymore, and I don't want that label." In sharing this, I'm not criticizing Narcotics Anonymous; it has helped many people overcome their addictions. I understand the need to accept responsibility and the reality that those who have been addicts can be prone to addictions. However, people haven't truly overcome the enemy and the specific struggle until they can shed the title that goes along with it. They have to be able to stand up and say, "My name is Luke. I am no longer a drug addict. I am a son, and I am so loved by my father."

A couple of years ago, Luke and my dad taught together about the prodigal son and the father for the first time. As I watched, I saw Luke stand with his hand extended, preaching the gospel, and I said to my dad, "There's the fulfillment of your vision." Now Luke, married with three children, is on our ministry staff and serving with us in Brazil. His testimony on the streets, in rescue homes, and in churches is powerful and full of the Father's compassion, love, and joy.

Luke learned that his identity was not in his bad actions, and he also learned that his identity could never be in his good actions. Even obedience does not determine our value. It's important, but it's not our identity. Only our identity as sons and daughters gives us value. If it was the other way around, Jesus never would have died for us while we were still sinners. But He did (see Rom. 5:8). He died for us in our worst moments so that we can live for Him in abundant life. Our identity is rooted in His love for and compassion toward us, as His children, not in our performance.

If our identity is sustained by our good behavior, when we have a bad day or our good works fail, our identity falls apart, too. This is not the way to the abundant life. Rather, our behavior should be in response to our identity as sons and daughters. A child desires to make the Father happy, not in order to earn His love but because the child is already loved. On the outside, the actions can look the same, but the Father sees our hearts. He is always beckoning us to walk with Him in sonship.

My two sons, Christian and Forrest, have illustrated this to me well. Sometimes they will be doing the same action—maybe cleaning their room or washing the dishes. However, one is doing it because he knows he is loved and wants to please his father, and the other is doing it because he feels that he has to earn my love—maybe because he got into trouble or is comparing himself to his brother. When I see that in one of my sons, I will pull him aside and ask, "What can you do to make your daddy love you more?"

I've asked each of my children this question a thousand times so they know the answer, "Nothing."

"And what can you do to make me love you less?"

Again he'll answer, "Nothing."

Then I'll hug him and hold him and tell him how much I love him. Even though I have asked my sons that question a thousand times, hearing it again immediately brings them back to a place of knowing who they are in their father. As sons and daughters, our behavior should not be motivated by what we can earn but by who we are and who we love.

His Favorite Song

This truth became much more real to me several years ago, while I was leading worship at one of Randy Clark's Schools of Healing and Impartation. Right in the middle of the event, on Saturday morning, I got sick and lost my voice. That's never a good thing for a worship leader. That afternoon, in a moment alone with the Lord, I said to Him, "I'm so glad that You love my worship even when I can't sing."

His response brought tears to my eyes. He said, "Nic, my favorite songs are sung by the mute."

The rest of the day, I was so captivated by the depth of the Father and His compassion, by the way His grace steps into our lives and turns our ashes into beauty. That night when we led worship, Rachael sang most of the songs, but when we sang the song, "Shores of Grace," my voice came back—only for that song. At the end of the song, as we lingered in the presence of God, I started to spontaneously sing these words:

You dance in the paintings of the blind.
You dwell in the melodies of the mute.
You're revealed in the suffering of the sick.
You rejoice in the fellowship of the poor.
Show us how to love like You love.

This prophetic song, which reveals so much about our Father's heart, changed my life. When we go to the streets, we are surrounded by depravity and weakness. We encounter pain that is almost incomprehensible. Walking those streets can feel very overwhelming—to me. But to my Father, the brokenness of the streets is simply a gigantic opportunity for compassion. He loves nothing more than to show Himself strong and loving and gracious in the midst of our weakness and pain. The story for all of God's children is the same. He meets us in our dirtiness and weakness; He heals us through His love; and then His strength in us reaches out to others, and we become living encounters with His compassion. Once we experience the Father's embrace, we become His embrace to the lost and broken.

You're After Our Hearts

By Nic and Rachael Billman

Come and wash me in Your name
Come and wash me in Your name
Come and bathe me in the fragrance
Overwhelm me in the presence

You're after our hearts
You're after our hearts
You're after our hearts again

You keep chasing after me,
And I keep letting You catch me
Ain't nothing gonna hold me back.
I'm coming Papa, I'm coming Daddy

I'm after Your heart
I'm after Your heart
I'm after Your heart again

CHAPTER FIVE

He's After Our Hearts

For God did not send His Son into the world to condemn the world, but that the world through Him might be saved.

—John 3:17

⟨ornament⟩

owntown Curitiba has a strip club, The Wiskaria, where our team has ministered many times. It all began one night as we walked the streets. I approached the bouncer to the club and asked if I could pray for him. He acted awkwardly, telling me he was a Christian and only worked there because he needed money. Then he proceeded to show me all of the Christian music on his phone to prove his story. Clearly, he had immediately started to feel guilty because he knew that this job was not God's will for him. However, I said, "It's no problem. God sees your heart, and He will provide another job for you, but in the meantime, He's here with you, and He loves you." That night we prayed with him, and he said he felt peace and a heat all over his body as we prayed, even though it was very cold that night.

The next time we came back, he had a big smile on his face, and he told us to wait out front. He went into the club and brought out five other bouncers, pointing to each one and declaring their need for prayer. "This one needs healing. This one just got divorced, and he's sad. This one doesn't know Jesus. This one has a problem with alcohol. And this one just needs a blessing." We prayed for each one, and as we prayed, some of the dancers came out to see what was going on. The girls on our team then talked and prayed with them. Even some clients saw us, came out to ask what we were doing, and then requested prayer—at a strip club!

As we were talking, the manager pulled up, and I thought we were in trouble because there was quite a commotion in front of his club. Leo, our bouncer friend, explained who we were, and the manager then asked for prayer as well. Then he said, "You are welcome to come to my club and pray for my employees anytime you want to." Shortly after that, we started sending a few of our girls into the club to pray for the dancers before and after their routines and to share about Jesus with them. While the girls were inside, we guys stayed outside and continued to love on Leo, the other bouncers, and the clients. We saw lots of inner healing and restoration take place both inside and outside of that club. In the months following, we introduced many of our friends and family to Leo at The Wiskaria, and every time he would request prayer. Eventually, God provided another job for Leo, but while he worked at The Wiskaria, God used him to open the door wide for encounters with His grace.

Jesus loved hanging out with people like Leo and the employees and patrons of The Wiskaria. He spent time with many sinners and outcasts—and it wasn't because He wanted to tell them they were wrong. Rather, compassion drove Jesus's interactions with people; He was after their hearts. This shouldn't surprise us, since Jesus was the exact representation of the compassionate Father (see Heb. 1:3). He approached every person He met from His heart. He saw their brokenness, and like His Father, He didn't focus on their actions but on the cry of their hearts. This love was the spark that started a great fire in people's hearts—that has since leapt from heart to heart to heart for thousands of years; it is the foundation of His Kingdom.

As missionaries, we have cried out every day for healing and freedom in Brazil. Our hearts are full of dreams for this nation. Yet we have learned that if we want the nation, we must first love individuals. As Heidi Baker, missionary to Mozambique, says, "You need to stop and love the one."[1] The keys to the nation are found in the one. If we want to see this nation in revival, we must love the one who is before us. Isaiah 60:22 says it this way, *"A little one shall become a thousand, and a small one a strong nation. I, the Lord, will hasten it in its time."* When we see the little one, we are staring at the multitude, and when we see the small one, we are staring at the nation.

This is the way that Jesus loved the nations. As He hung on the cross, He saw the multitudes. He saw the nations. But in the midst of the crowd, He also saw our faces. He saw me, and He saw you, and He said, "It's all for you!" Jesus had His Father's heart to see the many *and* to see the one. And over and over, throughout His ministry on earth, He stopped to love the one.

He Stopped for Her

The story of the Samaritan woman is one of my favorites (see John 4). She knew all about brokenness, and she was ripe for a heavenly encounter. Then she ran into Jesus, waiting alone at the well while His disciples purchased food. When she showed up to draw water, Jesus asked her for some. She, of course, was shocked. In that day, this encounter never should have happened. Yet despite all the cultural norms that should have made this meeting impossible, Jesus the Rabbi found Himself alone at Jacob's well with a woman of bad reputation. It was a divine set-up.

We know the story well. Jesus and the woman dialogue back and forth about the water and His surprising offer of "living water," but the woman doesn't seem to be taking Him seriously until Jesus announces His knowledge of her brokenness. In response to His command to "Go and get your husband," the woman replies, "I have no husband" (see John 4:16-17). Then Jesus uncovers her secret pain—"That is correct," Jesus responds, "because you have had five and the man that you are with now is not even your husband" (see John 4:17-18). Now He has her attention!

We don't know the cause of her five divorces, but we do know that in their culture she did not have the right to divorce her husband; only the husband could divorce the wife. The truth is, the cause doesn't matter; this woman had been badly hurt and rejected. I suspect that she, like many hurting people, had hardened her heart toward love and freedom, fearing further rejection. Then Jesus used a word of knowledge to penetrate the walls she had built around her heart.

Truth and Love

He spoke the truth, and He spoke it in love. This is the Jesus way to pursue people's hearts. Most of us, if we received a word of knowledge about five previous marriages and a current broken relationship, would ease into it very gently. We'd say something like, "I get the sense that you've been in some broken relationships." But Jesus told the woman to get her husband, knowing that this would provoke truth inside of her. At that, Jesus went right for it, pointing out her five ex-husbands and her current extramarital relationship. I used to feel uncomfortable just reading this Scripture because I kept thinking about how people might respond if I ever did something like that. I took my focus from the truth, assuming love and truth were mutually exclusive. But they're not, as Jesus shows us quite clearly. When we focus on truth *and* speak in love, even difficult subjects and sensitive issues will be overcome.

On the streets of Brazil, we have to walk in both truth and love continually because many of the people we minister to are great actors. People in prostitution are paid to act; they are paid to tell their clients what they want to hear. We have found that they are very good at acting with us as well. This is why we must listen to the voice of truth, even when the voice of circumstance is the more obvious of the two. One night we were talking with a girl who was about twenty-four years old. We asked her why she was in prostitution, and she told us it was because she liked the excitement and the money. "I love being a prostitute," she said.

As she was talking, I had a vision of her as a little girl singing on a stage in an empty room and then a quick vision of her hiding in a closet. I looked her in the eyes and said, "I don't believe you."

She assured me that she really did love prostituting.

I told her, "No little girl wants to be a prostitute when she grows up. I believe that you had a dream to sing, but no one would listen. I saw a vision of you singing on a stage in an empty room."

As tears began to fill her eyes, she said, "That actually happened. I was singing at my school, but not one of my family members came to hear me sing."

Then I shared the vision about the closet. I said, "I could be wrong, but I feel like there were times when you had to hide in your closet because you didn't feel safe."

She shared with us that she had been repeatedly raped by her step-father, and often she would hide in her closet without breathing in hopes that he wouldn't find her. That night we had a chance to pray with her and break off some of the shame and pain that she had experienced. Now she is in college, attending classes.

It's the truth that sets us free, and if we give people anything other than the truth, we are robbing them of their freedom. Simply agreeing with circumstance or condition is a form of pity, and it doesn't set a person free. But when we see with the eyes of compassion, when we are in pursuit of people's hearts, we will recognize the circumstance and condition, but look beyond them to the truth so that we can draw that truth out.

The Father doesn't ignore our pain or our struggle, but what He sings over us is our identity and our destiny. He is always declaring the truth, right through sin and circumstance, and He longs to draw the truth out of the hidden places of our hearts. That's what Jesus did with the woman at the well. He lovingly told her the truth about her circumstances and pain, removing the mask she was hiding behind, in order to introduce her to the truth of who she really was.

The Love Bulldozer

However, right in the midst of this soul-searching moment, she did something interesting. Just as Jesus was getting to her heart, she inserted a religious argument into the conversation in an attempt to divert His focus from her heart. She said, "Our fathers worshipped on this mountain, and you Jews say that you must worship in the temple in Jerusalem" (see John 4:20). We see this time and time again as we reach out to broken people. As we bring the truth of the Kingdom and the love of the Father, they throw up religious walls from previous hurt and rejection.

When loving broken people like Jesus did, we will encounter walls of offense. And we can handle them the same way He did. When the Samaritan woman brought up this religious question that had separated the Jews and Samaritans for so long, Jesus brought out His love bulldozer and plowed right through the walls! Jesus said, "Listen, the hour is coming and has now come, when it won't matter where you worship, but how you worship. True worshippers will worship the Father in spirit and in truth. God is Spirit, and those who worship Him must worship in spirit and truth" (see John 4:21-24). That's the sound of the walls of religion crumbling under the weight of the Father's heart!

It may seem ordinary to us, but in Jesus's day, this statement was revolutionary. Both Jews and Samaritans had strict rules defining what worship was, how to worship, and where to worship. Those rules had been distorted and perverted and had created such a distance between the Father and His children in worship. Jesus came to bridge that gap and bring the children back to the Father. We know that now, but at that time, Jesus's words were extremely bold and liberating.

The woman picked up on the liberating nature of this man and said, "I know that a Messiah, called Christ, is coming" (see John 4:25).

Jesus replied, "I who speak to you am He" (see John 4:26).

At these words, the woman believed Jesus, and she went back to her city to tell the news. Because of her testimony, most of the city believed in Jesus, too. All this happened because of a simple word of knowledge and the kindness with which Jesus pursued her heart. It wasn't as dramatic as we might expect, given the results. Jesus didn't heal her of blindness or deafness or walk on water to prove His Godhood. No, He simply became a friend to the friendless. He met this broken woman and spoke into her life. He used a word of knowledge to penetrate her heart and reveal her brokenness, and then He told her about her destiny. He said, "You are a true worshipper, and the Father loves your worship, because it is spirit and it is truth." He told her that if she drank of the living water, a fountain of everlasting life would flow from her, and that's exactly what happened.

She went back to her city, stood up in the town square, and told anyone who would listen about her encounter with the Messiah, Jesus. The Bible tells us that when they heard her testimony, they believed. Her testimony was so simple, yet so beautiful. She said, "He told me everything about myself" (see John 4:39). Her simple testimony compelled them to embrace Jesus because they saw the shimmer of transformation and the glow of love on her face. This woman had a bad reputation, but suddenly they saw freedom and love in her eyes, and they could not deny the truth of her words. She had been transformed by her encounter with Jesus, the Messiah.

Though she is often overlooked as such, this woman was one of the greatest evangelists recorded in the New Testament. She led nearly her whole city to Jesus. Yet we know very few details about her—not even her name—and she never resurfaces in the Bible. The point is: One of the greatest evangelists recorded in the New Testament was a woman whose simple testimony was, "He loves me!"

In Pursuit of Our Hearts

When we read stories like the Samaritan woman's, we see that Jesus always focused on people's hearts. When He met that woman, He wasn't interested in her past, her gifts, or what she could do for Him. He was interested in penetrating her heart because He knew that true transformation takes place in the heart and grows from the inside out. Often, when we're on the streets, one of the first things I will tell a woman in prostitution is, "I don't want anything from you, and I'm not going to ask you to do anything." Then I will tell her what God thinks about her and how He values her.

If we approach a woman in prostitution with the goal of conversion—instead of revealing her value through love—we may appear no different than one of her clients. To her, it seems like we are only interested in relationship with her because of what we can get out of her. If we are reaching out to the lost with the goal of leading them in a prayer or bringing them to church, our goals are too low. Jesus never tried to reach a quota. He didn't chase testimonies. He didn't need miracles to boost His self-image. Certainly, He loved testimonies and enjoyed operating in the wonderworking power of God, but His goal was nothing less than penetrating the hearts of people with the everlasting love of the Father.

An Honorable Trade

In 2009, Rachael and I had an experience in Curitiba, Brazil, that illustrates well the priority that Jesus placed on people's hearts. We were participating in an event led by Randy Clark called "Youth Power Invasion." One day, during our time there, we took a small team to minister around the city. We prayed for many people on the streets and in their homes, and a few people even stopped in their cars and requested prayer. When we approached one woman and asked if she needed healing for anything, she told us that she didn't, but her brother did. She led us around the corner to the three-room house where she, her parents, and her brother and his wife and daughter all lived. The mother told us that her son had had two strokes about seven years before. Since then, he had not been able to walk without arm-brace crutches, and his speech was very slurred.

We prayed for his healing, but after thirty minutes, the only result was that he felt more strength in his hands. Both Rachael and I felt that God was going to do something, so we continued praying and asking God to show us His heart. A little while later, Rachael looked up and saw a painting on the wall that had an evil-looking eye watching over a small city with a cross on one hill and a satanic symbol on another hill. She politely said, "That's an interesting painting you have there. Do you mind me asking the story behind it?"

As she said that, the man's mother began yelling. At the time, we didn't understand Portuguese so we had to wait for the translation. Eventually, we found out that she was yelling at her son, "I told you to get rid of that evil thing! I told you!" She then shared that a year earlier an evangelist had visited their church and told them that three items with demonic attachment in their house were keeping him from being healed. They had destroyed the other two, but the man did not want to get rid of the painting. He told us that he had bought it the year before his stroke for five reais from a drug-addicted painter who had consecrated it to satan.

I asked, "Are you willing to destroy it?"

He quickly said, "No."

As we prayed some more, I looked around the house and realized that this man owned nothing. For whatever reason, he loved this painting, and it was one of his few possessions. Now we wanted to take it away from him. So I asked him, "Would you trade me that painting for my watch?"

That was a surefire way to change the atmosphere! He quickly accepted .my offer and smiled proudly as I put the watch on his wrist. I traded a $150 watch for a $5 demonic painting, but the return on that investment was amazing. We took the painting outside, broke it in half, and threw it in a river. When we came back in, we led the family in a quick prayer renouncing any demonic attachment. Immediately the man's speech was restored, and we helped him stand up. Then he walked across the room without his arm-brace crutches for the first time since his stroke. He was even able to pick up his little daughter, who had been born right after the stroke, for the very first time.

When we see a person in affliction, whether it be sickness, depression, anxiety, or something else, we must learn to see with the eyes of Jesus. In the case of this man, we saw the physical condition, and we prayed accordingly, but it wasn't until we saw with Jesus's eyes that the true cause was revealed.[2] As we saw with Jesus's eyes, we not only saw the issue, but we also saw the man's heart. We recognized the value he had for this one possession, and rather than humiliating him, we were able to honor him with our trade. In the end, we introduced him to freedom in a way that told him, very tangibly, about his value and identity in his Father's eyes. This is always Jesus's priority. He's after our hearts, and He doesn't force our hand or humiliate us; He woos us with His kindness.

Let Love Lead

In this way, Jesus walked from town to town, loving the one in front of Him, and healings and miracles followed Him wherever He went. In all He did, He led with His heart. He expects us to do the same. In fact, He gave one of His strongest warnings about allowing our gifts to lead, rather than love:

> Not everyone who says to Me, "Lord, Lord," shall enter the kingdom of heaven, but he who does the will of My Father in heaven. Many will say to Me in that day, "Lord, Lord, have we not prophesied in Your name, cast out demons in Your name, and done many wonders in Your name?" And then I will declare to them, "I never knew you; depart from Me, you who practice lawlessness" (Matt. 7:21-23).

These people Jesus mentions will be believers who are doing the works of the Kingdom in the name of Jesus, but they are not true followers of Christ. The Greek word used for "knew" is *ginóskó*, and in this case, it's being used in reference to friendship.[3] Jesus was saying, "You are not my friends; we do not have relationship together." They were doing the works of the Kingdom apart from the heart of the Father—which is an illegitimate experience. It doesn't mean that the healings and miracles were fake, but just that, in relationship to their hearts, it was illegitimate.

Shortly after God called us to move to Brazil, I was praying in my office at our church, and I heard the Lord say, "Nic, if you let your faith increase above your love, you become dangerously close to, 'Depart from me; I never knew you.'" That was one of the most transformational moments of my life. Over the next several weeks, the Holy Spirit took me on a journey of discovering the relationship between the compassion of Jesus and the faith of those He encountered.

At the end of First Corinthians 13, Paul said, *"And now abide faith, hope, love, these three; but the greatest of these is love"* (1 Cor. 13:13). Faith and hope are both rooted in love. Throughout Jesus's ministry, He showed compassion to the sick and broken; then after they were healed, He said, "Your faith has made you well." We do not read much about the faith of Jesus, but we read a lot about the compassion and love of Jesus.

One example of this is found in Mark 10, when Bartimaeus called out, *"Jesus, Son of David have mercy on me!"* Jesus heard his cries, stopped, and called Bartimaeus to Him. When Jesus asked him what he wanted, he said he wanted to see.

In response, Jesus said, *"…Your faith has made you well,"* and immediately Bartimaeus was healed.

Then there's the leper in Luke 17. People who had leprosy were usually rejected and abandoned by society at large. Instead, they lived in communities of lepers or in complete isolation. But Jesus wasn't afraid of leprosy; He approached the ten lepers and gave them a command to go to the priests. As they went, they were healed, but only one of them returned to give thanks to Jesus. When he returned, Jesus said, *"…Your faith has made you well"* (Luke 17:19). Lastly, the woman who had the issue of blood was physically healed, then her place among her people was restored, and then Jesus said, *"…Your faith has made you well…"* (Luke 8:48).

In these stories we see that faith is a natural response to compassion.

When Jesus prioritized people's hearts and treated them with compassion, they responded to Him in faith, and as a result, miracles happened. We see this quite often on the streets. When we first approach people on the streets, often they think it is a joke or that we are going to make fun of them. But once they look into our eyes and see genuine care and compassion, they have more faith to listen and believe what we are saying. Many times our nights are spent simply listening to the broken hearts of the people on the streets and looking them in the eyes as we tell them, "You are so loved by Father God."

When people looked into the eyes of Jesus, they saw true love burning through all of the lies. They saw a compassion that was deeper than any pity they had ever received. Because of His radical compassion, faith increased inside of them, enabling them to believe what He said. As a result, many of them left everything behind and followed Him. The same will happen as we look with His eyes and pursue the hearts of people with the same compassion that Jesus had. In Mark 16:17-18, Jesus promised that signs and wonders will follow those who believe. And in John 14:12, He promised that we will do the works that He did and even greater works. As we walk side-by-side with Jesus on the streets of this world, choosing to see the multitudes and the individuals through His eyes of compassion, signs and wonders *will* follow us. This is the key. We must let love lead.

PART TWO

Sing Me Like a Song

By Nic and Rachael Billman

The sound of a thousand dove's wings in flight
The sound of many waters rushing over and o'er
The sound of Heaven's keys dancing in the night
The sound of a Father, the song of a Son
The roar of a Lion, the breath of a Lamb
The sound of the harvest receiving the wind

My lover, I am Yours.
So sing me like a song.
However and whenever You want.
Just sing me like a song.

The sound of Your breakers colliding the shore
The cry of the deep, the beckon of love
The shackles and chains falling down to the floor
The sound of Your heartbeat calling me home
The sound of our tears filling bottles of clay
The dropping of blood on stones meant for us

My lover, I am Yours.
So sing me like a song.
However and whenever You want.
Just sing me like a song.

CHAPTER SIX

The Ultimate Tuning Fork

*The LORD your God in your midst, The Mighty One,
will save; He will rejoice over you with gladness, He will quiet you
with His love, He will rejoice over you with singing.*

—Zephaniah 3:17

⟶ ☙ ❧ ⟵

In July of 2010, while we were in Santa Fe, New Mexico, we had two amazing experiences in one day—one at the Plaza downtown (which I'll get to later) and one at a church we ministered at that night. At that church, at the end of our worship set, Rachael and I played our crystal bowls. And something beautiful happened. At first absolute silence filled the building. Then the first bowl chimed *dong*, and the sound of the deep swells began to grow. Then the second bowl, with a higher octave, chimed *dong*, and the sound of the two bowls filled the room. After a minute or two, a woman began to sing in the Spirit along with the bowls. Within five minutes, everyone in the room was singing in the spirit in perfect harmony with the bowls. It was a beautiful and holy moment.

In that moment the Holy Spirit began to pour revelation into my heart. I heard Him say, "These bowls are just like Jesus. He was sent to bring the sons and daughters and all of creation into harmony with the Father." In other words, Jesus was a song that God sang on the earth. God has always been a singing God, and the greatest song that He ever sang was Jesus. When He sent Jesus to earth, it wasn't just to die for our sins and redeem us; it was to show us how to live. He was sent to be the ultimate tuning fork that gave us the perfect key to live by. This is why the writer of Hebrews said we are to look to Jesus as the author and finisher of our faith. He was the perfect song sung by the Father to bring His children back to Him. Even on the cross, He sang to us in sweet surrender. Once we hear the song of Jesus, we fall in love with Him, and we join in the song. It's the greatest duet that ever existed, the Bridegroom and the Bride singing the love song of salvation and redemption.

The young girls in our rescue homes have heard the song of Jesus and have fallen in love with Him. They have tasted freedom, and they want others to experience the same freedom—even those who caused their bondage and pain. They have come into perfect harmony with the redemption song of Jesus, and they sing it daily, not just with their mouths, but also with their lives. My friend Randy Clark, who knew John Wimber personally, often quotes Wimber as having said, "God, I want to be a coin in Your pocket; spend me however You want."[1] What a simple yet profound prayer! Because I'm a musician, my prayer is, "God, let me be a song in Your heart; sing me however You want."

Made to Create

When we find the right pitch and join in eternity's song, our lives begin to create a melody that literally shifts atmospheres everywhere we go. Like the crystal bowls, the beauty of our duet with Heaven changes environments and points people's hearts toward the Father. We can do this because our Father made us in His image, and like Him, we are made to create. In Genesis, we read that God created all things with the sound of His voice— except humanity. When he created Adam, he molded him with His hands and then breathed life, His Spirit, into him. After he created Adam, God did something surprising; He brought all the animals He had created to Adam to see what he would call them (see Gen. 2:19). In other words, He invited Adam into the creative process.

God didn't have predetermined names selected for the animals. He didn't give Adam a book of the 1,001 most popular animal names to choose from. Rather, I picture God sitting with Adam, listening as he says, "I'll call this one a duck," and laughing as He watches His new son enjoy His creation. I believe God asked Adam to name the animals because creating and naming was part of his DNA. He was created in the image of his Father, who spoke all things into existence, and now he too would speak the identity of the animals into existence. This causes me to wonder: *Did Adam name the animals based on their characteristics, or did the animals obtain their characteristics because of the names Adam gave them?*

Just like Adam, we have been created in the image of our Papa, and we too have the ability to create and to speak realities into existence. As we talked about in Chapter 3, we have the power to speak identity into others. Similarly, we also have the power to create change and to shift atmospheres. We are to see things the way that God sees them and declare them as such. God never intended for us to simply be reactive people, responding to the circumstances of life and the attacks of the enemy. Rather, in the same way that God created the universe from nothing, He has placed His creative character inside of us so that we too can see with the proactive eyes of creativity, enabling us to declare destiny and to shift atmospheres. We call things that are not as though they are, and we speak life into dry bones (see Heb. 11:3; Ezek. 37). However, we don't shift atmospheres only with our words. As we see in the life of Jesus, our worship and our service play a very big role in our ability to bring the climate of Heaven down to earth.

Worship Changes Things

First, let's talk about worship. *Worship* is another word for *surrender*. When we worship, we say, "You are worthy of all of me, and I place my will at Your feet." God is not only our Father; He is also our King, and being part of His Kingdom means worshipping Him, not only with our mouths but with lives of surrender. Jesus, the firstborn Son, modeled this so completely in His life of doing only what the Father said and in His death on the cross. In this way, He transformed a symbol of death into the symbol of love, freedom, and redemption. His act of worship changed everything.

To fully understand Jesus's life of worship, we must answer this question: *What actually killed Jesus?* Some say it was the sins of humanity, separation from the Father, or the torture and crucifixion itself. But none of those things killed Jesus. Surrender killed Jesus. Jesus plainly said that no one could take His life from Him, but that He had the authority to lay it down (see John 10:18). This is why He didn't die until He said, *"Father, into Your hands I commit My spirit"* (Luke 23:46). Surrender brought the completion of God's will for Jesus's natural life on earth. Surrender finalized the old covenant and established the new covenant. The sacrifice of worship that Jesus gave His Father when He died on the cross—literally surrendering His life—eternally shifted the atmosphere of the earth.

We too have the ability and the call to shift atmospheres through our worshipful surrender. Jesus is the great model, and He said that following Him means denying ourselves and taking up our cross daily (see Luke 9:23). In other words, we must daily surrender our wills and our plans to the plan of our Father, and we must choose to walk with Him on the streets of this life, wherever He may lead us. This is the key to the supernatural lifestyle. When we surrender our wills, we allow the Father's will to be done in our lives. When we worship Him with our lives, everything around us changes.

Living as Thermostats

Now I will tell you about the other amazing encounter we had with Jesus in Santa Fe, New Mexico. It shows the power of worship to shift atmospheres, even in the darkest of places. While we were in town, our dear friend, Alan Hawkins, wanted to show us the Plaza in Santa Fe, which is basically a town square with a large yard, some trees, and a large monument in the middle. It's a gathering place for both locals and tourists and a popular place to pray, play, and smoke weed. Santa Fe is essentially the New Age and spiritual capital of the western United States, hosting a fusion of the New Age, eastern religions, Wicca, and Native American spiritual beliefs. It is a melting pot of syncretism and a gathering place of seekers—and the Plaza is one of its spiritual hubs.

As Alan parked the car, I noticed a guy playing a beat-up guitar and singing through a mic that was plugged into an amp powered by a car battery. He had a hat in front of him to collect money, and he was singing a mixture of sixties folk songs and his own original songs. During a break from his singing, I went over and asked him if I could play a song. At first he was hesitant, but after I slipped him a twenty-dollar bill, his vision was transformed, and he was happy to oblige. As I started to play, Rachael came over and joined me. We sang a song we wrote called "Sing Me Like a Song." To those who don't know us, it might seem like a simple poetic love song. As we sang, a crowd began to gather, and many people were putting money in the man's hat.

When the song was over, I thanked him and attempted to give him his guitar back, but he was a smart businessman. He saw the money overflowing from the hat, and he asked us to play another song. The second song we sang was "Shores of Grace." Again, those who don't know the purpose for which we write could think it's just a beautiful song about a father and his love. As we sang, the crowd grew even larger. Again, after the song, I tried to give the guitar back to the man, but he was counting bills, so he said, "Keep playing!" This time we played a song called "The Invitation," in which we sing the name of Jesus three times.

As we sang the song, we could feel the Holy Spirit's presence thickening, and when we got to the part of the song with the name of Jesus, hands went up all around the Plaza, and some began to cry. Our simple song of worship and our obedience to follow the Father's lead had introduced a new climate to the Plaza. Jesus was in the park! And though the people were involved in the New Age, eastern religion, and witchcraft, suddenly, they were worshipping the name of Jesus. Though they served false gods, they were all seekers, and Jesus promises that if we seek Him we will find Him. All of the people on the Plaza that day are sons and daughters created by the hands and the breath of their Father, and as our worship shifted the atmosphere, they were able to respond to the sound of their Father calling their names.

After we were done, we thanked the man who owned the guitar, and as we got up to leave, we were greeted by several people from the crowd. One guy who had long dreadlocks and sported the unique fragrance of marijuana said, "Thank you! That was such a positive spirit."

I hugged him and said, "You have no idea how positive He is."

Several other people simply asked us, "What was that?"

We told them, "It's Jesus, and He loves you very much."

One young lady came to Rachael and asked her to pray with her. She was a vocalist and had been dabbling in Hinduism, but had not felt peace for a long time. She said that when we sang, she felt peace return to her. Rachael had a chance to pray with her and share a prophetic word that God had for her. The girl just wept and wept, and then she gave her heart to Jesus and smiled and smiled. It was beautiful.

That day we worshipped the Father, He came and inhabited our praise (see Ps. 22:3), and the atmosphere changed. We are not created to be thermometers; we are created to be thermostats. Thermometers simply gauge the temperature, but thermostats change the temperature. It's easy to look at a place like Santa Fe and say, "Look at all of this syncretism. Look at all of these false gods and evil practices." That takes no talent or spiritual gifting at all. However, we aren't created to make a list of all that is wrong in an atmosphere; we are created to change the atmosphere. That's what Jesus did. He looked with the eyes of the Father, and then He changed atmospheres by living a life of worship and surrender.

This Smells Like You

My daughter, Leila, is seven years old, and she has a blankey that has been around since the day she was born. It has been left in hotels, it has been drug through the mud, and it has travelled the world. Leila loves her blankey. One day she came to me, holding just a corner of the blankey, and she said, "Daddy, this part smells like you, and whenever I miss you, I smell this part of blankey, and I feel like you're close."

Worship is like this; we come so close to the Father that we smell like Him. Then, wherever we go, we carry His fragrance, and the people around us can sense His presence. This reminds me of the time when the sinful woman anointed Jesus's feet (see Luke 7:36:50). Jesus and His disciples were eating at a Pharisee's house when this woman entered the room and poured out her worship by anointing Jesus's feet with perfumed oil. Suddenly the atmosphere changed. The whole house was filled with the fragrance of her worship. Though the perfume was poured out only on Jesus—He was the focus—the whole house was filled with the fragrance. Everyone left smelling like Jesus—even those who were casting judgment.

In the same way, when we fix our eyes on Jesus and pour our worship out on Him, holding nothing back, the atmosphere begins to transform. When I talk about worship, I'm not just talking about music. Songs and dances alone won't change the atmosphere. The sinful woman didn't sing a song; she washed Jesus's feet with her tears, wiped them with her hair, and anointed them with expensive oil. In other words, her worship cost her. It was a surrender of her heart to Jesus, and it is that sort of surrender—whether it includes singing or not—that transforms atmospheres. Jesus didn't die on the cross so that we could sing good songs in church services. He died on the cross so that we could live lifestyles of worship, lifestyles that bring His presence wherever we go.

Becoming the Outpouring

Now, let's talk about service. Our worship and the surrender of our hearts are aimed at the Father. Our service is aimed at the people He loves. It is the other half of the atmosphere-shifting strategy that Jesus modeled:

Jesus, knowing that the Father had given all things into His hands, and that He had come from God and was going to God, rose from supper and laid aside His garments, took a towel and girded Himself. After that, He poured water into a basin and began to wash the disciples' feet, and to wipe them with the towel with which He was girded (John 13:3-5).

This wrecks me! The Father had given all things into Jesus's hands; He had all authority and all power. Yet He recognized that the other half of worshipping His Father is serving the ones He loves. In preparation for the greatest atmosphere change in history, Jesus did the unexpected with His authority. He took off His outer garments and positioned Himself in the lowest place in the room. In those days, washing feet was the job of a servant; because people wore sandals and walked on dusty roads, a basin of water and a towel were always placed by the door for when guests arrived. Though it wasn't His duty, Jesus chose to serve; He took off His garments and clothed Himself with the towel of a servant.

But this wasn't the first time Jesus stooped low for others. As He walked the streets of His world, He continually poured Himself out, with love and compassion, to all He met. He poured out wine and said, "Take and drink," and ultimately, He poured out His blood on the cross. That night, He poured out water to wash the feet of His disciples. Though He was the King of all, Jesus chose to serve others, and as He poured Himself out in service, He changed atmospheres with His love. This is what it looks like to be a leader in God's family. This is what it takes to shift atmospheres and introduce the lost to the voice of their Father. It takes a love that serves, even when it doesn't have to.

This is why, as a leader for our ministry, my place is serving at the feet of our staff. Rachael and I have a calling on our lives to elevate others into their destinies. We desire that, one day, a huge pile of people will be reaching toward the sky, and at the very bottom of the pile, we'll be standing with big smiles on our faces. The place of a pastor is not ruling over the heads of the people but serving at the feet of the people. The first step toward becoming a great leader is grabbing a towel and a basin of water—not a microphone. Even the world understands the importance of servant leadership in our ability to create change. Years ago, when I worked in human resources and mortgage finance for a seven billion dollar corporation, I observed some great men and women who truly understood what it means to be a leader. The best leaders are the ones who realize their job is not to control their people, but to serve them by equipping and motivating them to be their best. Jesus modeled this when there was no precedent. He was the great forerunner, and as His followers, we too must be quick to serve. Pouring out our lives for others is one of the great keys to changing realities and actually becoming an outpouring as we walk the streets of this life.

Just a few days after Jesus washed His disciples' feet, He poured Himself out on the cross. He surrendered His life in worship to the Father, and He poured out His life in service to humanity. With His mouth He spoke a new reality into existence, *"It is finished!"* (John 19:30). At that powerful synthesis of His worship, service, and declaration, the curtain of separation in the Temple was torn, and Jesus introduced the greatest atmosphere shift the world has ever seen.

Now that we have been washed by Jesus, we become part of His outpouring on the world. We get to shift hearts and atmospheres with Him. One night recently, I watched Rachael do just that. As she washed and anointed with oil the feet of one of our friends in prostitution, both women cried. As Rachael sang over her friend and washed her feet, Jesus washed the woman's shame and pain away. In this simple act, Rachael worshipped the Father and served a woman He loves. And as she sang the truth about her identity, the presence of Jesus came into the room.

Jesus once said, *"Freely you have received, freely give"* (Matt. 10:8). This is our invitation to be vessels in the hands of the Father who are filled up and poured out on the people who walk the streets of this world. This is our opportunity to align with the song of Heaven and bring the atmosphere of Heaven to earth. As Rachael likes to say, "God is not looking for vessels of gold or silver; He's just looking for willing vessels." Are you willing?

At Your Feet

By Nic and Rachael Billman

Lovely are the feet of the one who brings good news
You came to the earth and took a walk in my shoes
You walked upon the waves and dirty streets alike
You danced upon injustice and the enemy was under Your feet
Where are You walking today?
I want to walk with You.

Your feet are beautiful, Jesus
With the marks and scars of a journey and a cross
And with each step the fragrance of perfumes and sacrifice
And the holes in Your hands are big enough to swallow up all the pain on these
streets

The highest place is at Your feet
So I'll bring You my highest praise
Here at Your feet

CHAPTER SEVEN

Seeing Like Jesus

Greater love has no one than this, than to lay down one's life for his friends.

—John 15:13

*J*ust a few months ago, I was in a small park in Recife surrounded by street children and homeless adults. It was close to midnight, and in that park, little girls as young as ten were prostituting, and street boys of the same age were sniffing glue and smoking crack. Some people there have literally lost their minds because of drug and alcohol abuse and are now living homeless on the streets. At the edge of the park stood police, who often come to beat the children when they have nothing else to do. I sat right in the middle of the chaos. It was hardly the ideal soaking atmosphere with quiet instrumental music and meditative prayers; rather, it was loud with the sounds of the city and these broken people.

But Jesus comes right into the middle of our chaos and brokenness, our sin and suffering. God didn't dance around the edges; He put the cross right in the middle of it all. That night in Brazil, right in the middle of the chaos and brokenness, the Father asked me a question. He said, "Son, what do you see?" I knew God wanted to show me what He saw, so I waited and looked around the dirty little park. As I looked at the children, I saw them begin to bloom like flowers. I saw fruit trees springing up where there was only concrete and trash, and I saw a river begin to flow through the drugs and the violence.

I responded to the Lord, "I see a garden."

He replied, "Good! So do I."

As sons and daughters, this is what we do. The Father gives us seeds, and we plant them among the broken soil of our generation. He is always faithful to water the gardens we have planted.

The Holes in His Hands

One night I was sitting on the streets with a group of street children, and I had a vision. In the vision, Jesus came to me and said, "I want to show you how I see these children." We were sitting next to each other, and He held up His hand, still marked with a hole from the nail that had pierced it. When I looked through the hole in His hand, I saw the children differently; I saw them dancing and laughing, playing and singing. I could see their destinies being painted like a masterpiece painting, and I could feel the joy that He found in these precious ones (see Heb. 12:2). He said to me, "The holes in My hands are big enough to swallow up all of the pain on these streets."

When we rescue children and adults from prostitution, we're not rescuing them solely because of their condition. We're rescuing them because of their destiny. It's not enough to be sad about their condition or to want to rescue them because of their circumstances. We have to see them the way that the Father sees them. We have to see their destiny. When we do, we will be driven to rescue that destiny. When I look at the street children in Brazil, I see songs that haven't been written, paintings that have never been seen, business strategies that haven't been released, and cures for diseases. I see political leaders and missionaries of the Father's heart. That is what we are rescuing. When we look with His eyes, we see people by their destinies, we see them as friends, and we see them as family. We see like He sees.

Can These Bones Live?

An Old Testament story illustrates that God sees people according to their destinies, not according to their problems. In Ezekiel 37, the prophet Ezekiel finds himself in a valley of dry bones, quite literally surrounded by death and decay. Then God asks him a question, *"Can these bones live?"* (Ezek. 37:3).

It's always significant when God, the one who knows everything, asks a question. He does it because He is about to transform our vision. God's question stirs possibility in Ezekiel's heart, and he responds, *"Oh Lord God, You know"* (Ezek. 37:3). With one question, God shifts Ezekiel's perspective; what had seemed like an impossible situation transforms in the light of God's unlimited power. Suddenly, Ezekiel sees the potential for change hidden in God's heart.

God then directs Ezekiel to prophesy life and breath to the bones. As he does, the bones came to life, transforming into an *"exceedingly great army"* (Ezek. 37:10). The possibility became reality. And Ezekiel's vision was changed. God took him to the valley of dry bones because He wanted to transform the way he saw his nation and his generation. God does this sometimes. He puts us in the middle of a valley of death and ask us, "What do you see?" "Do you see dry bones and death, or do you see an army?"

Those dry bones had long been dead and forgotten, yet from them God chose to raise up an army. Their years of death did not cause God to lose sight of their potential or their destiny. Likewise, on the streets of this world, an army of lost souls waits for the mature sons and daughters of God to prophesy life and breath into them. The question is, what do we see—a pile of dry bones or a mighty army? The abandoned, the abused, the outcast, the trafficked, and the untouchable are the dry bones of our generation. They are a hungry army longing to be filled with something of substance—the breath of their Papa. God is calling us to stand amidst these dry bones and declare their value and their destiny. His goal is for us to see the way He sees, to see that nothing is impossible to those who believe and that dry bones really can stand up and walk (see Matt. 19:26; Mark 9:23).

Seeing the Untouchable

Not surprisingly, Jesus was quite good at seeing destiny in people who looked a lot like dry bones. In John 9 we find a story that illustrates that well. As Jesus approached a man who was born blind, His disciples asked Him, *"Rabbi, who sinned, this man or his parents, that he was born blind?"* (John

9:2). To us, this seems like a strange question. But in their culture, being born with a disability indicated a generational sin or curse. Such people were seen as being rejected by God; they were the ultimate outcasts. After all, why would people bother to care about someone God had rejected?

Many cultures today believe this very thing. I have visited Nepal twice, and I have seen the untouchables in the markets and streets begging for money. Untouchable children are told, from birth, that they are the lowest of the low. Some of them are not even given names, and they are taught not to make eye contact with a person of a higher caste because it would devalue that other person.

The belief system of the superstitious Jewish culture in the days of Jesus was similar. For example, beggars were given the garments of a beggar so that all would know they were beggars. Our clothing has a funny way of becoming our identity. Though wealthy people would give disabled beggars some coins, they would mock them by kicking dirt at them, throwing the offering in their faces, or spitting on them. They did this to show that, although they were giving an offering, they didn't want the curse to come upon their lives.

Once, when I was in Nepal, I saw a row of untouchables begging for money and food. Among them crouched a little untouchable beggar girl about nine years old. She was sitting on the ground with her hand out and her head down, refusing to make eye contact with people, even as they gave her a coin. As I watched, a well-dressed Nepalese woman came by and gave this girl a coin and then spat on her face. The little girl did not even wipe the spit from her face. She simply put the coin in her pocket and continued to beg. Her whole life she had been told "untouchable" was her value and identity. Being mocked and spit upon was her lot in life. Amazingly, Jesus Himself was mocked and spit upon right before He displayed the true value of people like that little girl on the cross.

This cultural perspective gives us a better understanding for why the disciples asked whose sin had caused the man's blindness. Jesus's response broke through that culture with compassion: *"Jesus answered, 'Neither this man nor his parents sinned, but that the works of God should be revealed in him'"* (John 9:3). Jesus looks at challenges differently than we do. We see a problem that needs to be fixed; Jesus sees an opportunity for God's love. He knows that no one is beyond His reach. No bones are too dry; no destiny is too buried. Jesus wasn't afraid of this man's problems because He knew what was possible with God. He looked with His heart.

Then Jesus did something radical. He spit on the ground, made mud, and put it on the eyes of the blind man. Then He told him to go wash his eyes. Jesus didn't do this just to spice up His healing routine. He did it with a very calculated purpose rooted in His love for the blind man and His recognition of the blind man's deepest need. See, the disciples saw blind eyes that needed healing, but Jesus looked deep into the heart of the man and saw a broken man who, since he was born, had been distinguished in his culture as a beggar and a sinner—a cursed man. All hope and destiny have been stripped from him, and he'd been mocked, mistreated, devalued, and even spit upon.

Now Jesus was face-to-face with this man, and He could have healed him in any way He wanted to. From His many options, Jesus chose to release healing through spit; the very thing that had been used to mock and devalue this man had become the tool of healing. As instructed, the man went to the pool of Siloam, washed, and returned with open eyes and a healed heart. People saw blind eyes, but Jesus saw deeper; He saw the man's true destiny, and He healed him in a way that also restored his value and his wounded heart. Throughout His life on earth, Jesus saw people according to their destiny, not their problems. He valued them for who they were created to be, and He imparted to them belief for the impossible.

Jesus, Friend of Sinners

Jesus also saw all people as His friends, as He epitomized in these words: *"Greater love has no one than this, than to lay down one's life for his friends"* (John 15:13). He laid His life down for all of us, and He chose to call us friends—even before we knew Him—*not* sinners. This is still how Jesus views the lost today. He does not view them as sinners who need to be rescued or as projects who need to be fixed; He views them as His friends, and He asks us to do the same.

One day not too long ago, we experienced this reality in a whole new way through the simplicity of our children and their propensity to view everyone as a friend. As a family, we were at the store buying groceries. At the time, our entire team of twenty people, including our family, lived in the same six-bedroom house. We didn't have a ministry center or building of any kind, so our ministry was either on the streets or in our home. As we were driving home from the store, one of our team members called and said, "Just wanted to let you know that Drika and Natalia are here at the house." Drika and Natalia are two of our friends from the streets of Curitiba that we had been building a great relationship with. At the time, they were both transvestites in prostitution, although Drika has since left the streets.

Our children had seen transvestites on the streets, and they had heard us talk about transvestites, but we had never had a talk explaining what that means. So Rachael and I had a parent whisper conversation in the front seat, strategizing for ten minutes about how we would explain what a transvestite is. After coming up with an in-depth plan and explanation, I began, "Kids, do you understand what a transvestite is?"

Forrest said, "Yeah, Dad. A transvestite is a boy who dresses like a girl because he doesn't know his identity."

To that I replied, "Uh, yeah. Good talk."

Children see things in simple ways, and that simplicity allows them to understand the deeper things without all of the complications, opinions, and prejudices. Without getting hung up on the particular sins, our boys were able to see through to the deeper issue—lost identity. This enabled them to view these people from the streets as *friends who don't yet know how valuable they are,* which is very much like God's perspective. As a result, their definition of *transvestite* was much better than the one I had prepared.

One of our closest friends in Brazil, Mara, is a woman who's been in prostitution for nearly half of her life. She is so close to being free, and she is going to the streets far less than she used to, but she is still in prostitution. When our youngest daughter, Cássia, was born, Mara was one of the first people to hold her. She is family, and our children love her. They don't see her as a project or even as a prostitute; they only see her as a friend.

This past summer, I had the purity talk with my boys when they were nine and ten years old. Because of the nature of what we do, they see and hear a lot of things that most boys their age are not exposed to. So Rachael and I felt it was time to explain the beauty of sex within marriage and how important purity is. Before this talk, their understanding of prostitution was basically that these are people who don't know how special they are so they let others hurt them. We were sitting in my truck in New Mexico, while visiting the United States, as I explained sex and purity to my sons. I explained that this is why what we do is so important because this gift of sexual purity is being stolen from the men, women, and children whom we love on the streets of Brazil.

Both of their faces got very sad, and they sat quietly. Tears began to form in Christian's eyes, and I could see that God was touching his little heart. He asked me, "Dad, is that what people are doing to Mara?"

I started to cry too, and I said, "Yes, buddy, that's why we're trying to help her see how special she is so she can be free."

Then Forrest, also with tears in his eyes and with a look of urgency asked, "Is that what people are doing to the children in our video? To children Leila's age?"

I said, "Yes, that's why we're opening homes for these children." That night my boys learned how special purity is. And they learned the importance of our fight for our friends. As we walk the streets of Brazil, we're not looking for sinners to condemn or convince; like Jesus, we're looking for friends, and when we find them, we tell them how beautiful and special they really are. We tell them that they're more valuable and important than they ever imagined, and we introduce them to their Father.

In Luke 19, we find an example of the way Jesus, as He walked the streets of life and called the lost to follow Him, was truly a friend to the friendless. It's the familiar story of Zacchaeus, the rich tax collector with a bad reputation who had been stealing money. When Zacchaeus heard Jesus was in town, he longed to see Him so much that he climbed a Sycamore tree in hopes of getting a better view. Seeing Zacchaeus in the tree, Jesus invited Himself to lunch at Zacchaeus's house. By doing this, Jesus claimed him as His friend. All the people began to question Jesus's choice for His new friend, but then something amazing happened. Stirred by the value that Jesus had placed on him by calling him "friend," Zacchaeus suddenly promised to give half of his earnings to the poor and to repay what he had stolen fourfold. Jesus didn't approach Zacchaeus with an agenda or stipulations for their relationship. He simply valued and embraced him based on his identity rather than his reputation; He simply called him "friend." As a result, on that day his entire family was saved.

The Place of Belonging

Reflecting on His encounter with Zacchaeus, Jesus said, *"The Son of Man has come to seek and to save that which was lost"* (Luke 19:10). By definition, for a person to be lost, that person, at some point previously, must have been found and must have belonged. In other words, He was looking for His long-lost friends. Once, after I prayed with a fifty-year-old man to receive Jesus for the first time, I told him, "Welcome back to the family."

With a confused look in his eyes he said, "Welcome back? But this is the first time that I've made this choice."

I laughed and replied, "Yes, but God chose you even before you were born and has been waiting with open arms for you to return to your place of belonging."

As we talked about in Chapter 1, we are all aware of this place of belonging—or the hunger for it inside our hearts. We were created as sons and daughters of God, and though many of us have wandered far from home, our hearts long for the place where we belong, for family. This is what causes lost people to act like Zacchaeus—a wealthy man in a prominent position who threw aside fear of embarrassment and rejection and climbed up a tree to see Jesus. He was driven by hunger and desperation, by the longing to find that place of belonging. I believe the lost truly are hungry and desperate for Jesus; most of them just don't know it yet. Most of them know *something* is missing. They feel tired of living in depression and loneliness. But they don't know Jesus is the answer. They've forgotten that God is their Father.

That's where we come in. We must first reveal the character of Jesus to the lost so they have a desire to know the man that character belongs to. We must show them what it's like to belong in His family, and we must treat them like the sons and daughters that they are. So many people have no idea who Jesus really is. They've been hurt or confused by religion, and they think Jesus is pointing at them in judgment. They desperately need to see who He really is. They need an encounter with the love and grace of the Son of God, who said, *"For God did not send His Son into the world to condemn the world, but that the world through Him might be saved"* (John 3:17).

This is what Jesus lived and preached while He walked this earth. Now it's our turn. As we see people the way Jesus sees them—as people with destiny, as friends, as family—we will be living encounters with His love, and we will get to witness the joyful reunion of the Father and His kids. We will see dry bones stand up as a mighty army. The Father is passionately pursuing the lost, and He wants the found to join in the pursuit.

Close to Your Heart

By Nic Billman

Hide me. Oh hide me,
In the shadow of Your wings,
In the sound of Your heartbeat,
Keep me. Keep me close,
Close to Your heart,
Is where I belong.

Close to Your heart is where I want to be.
Close to Your heart is where I belong.

And make me true in the deepest places.
Cause I want to know You,
To really know You, Lord.
Create in me a heart that is clean
And beats for You and You alone
And take not away Your Spirit from me
I long to be with you.

Close to Your heart is where I want to be.
Close to Your heart is where I belong.

CHAPTER EIGHT

Show Me How to Love

*"The thief does not come except to steal, and to kill,
and to destroy. I have come that they may have life,
and that they may have it more abundantly"*

—John 10:10

One Tuesday night not too long ago, we were at our street church in the little dirty park in downtown Recife. As our team sat on the ground with the children and adults in attendance, I walked around the park observing. I looked over at our group, and I saw a huge angel above them. I knelt down and began to pray, and when I looked back up, I realized that it wasn't one huge angel; it was many angels ascending and descending. Jesus is the ladder to Heaven, and angels ascend and descend upon Him (see John 1:51). Because He dwells in us, angels ascend and descend upon our lives. This means that we have continual access to Heaven because of Christ living in us.

As I was watching, I heard the Holy Spirit say, "All of creation is groaning and waiting for the revealing of the sons of God" (see Rom. 8:19). At that moment, I looked up and noticed the trees in the park—a park where robbery, bloodshed, rape, and murder are common. I thought, *I wonder what these trees have seen? Certainly they have seen many things that are a far cry from the destiny of God's children.* Yet these trees were created in God's glory, in Christ and through Christ (see John 1:3), and they are part of the joint longing of creation for the revelation of God's children. As I considered this, I realized that Christ in me is the hope of glory. In other words, the desire of the nations and the longing of creation is fulfilled within me—within each of the redeemed. So as a prophetic act for our precious ones in the park and our city, I laid my hands on each tree, saying, "The Bible says that you are groaning and waiting for the revealing of the mature sons of God. I know the things you've seen, but I'm here to tell you that I'm what you've been waiting for. Just wait and see what my Papa will do in this place!"

The very next Sunday, while I was ministering at a church in São Paulo, the worship team sang a song that says, "Take me to the high places." The Lord began to show me a vision of "the high places"; I was overcome and knelt down on the ground in tears. He showed me how he walked among the little prostitutes and murderers at our street church, and I saw His feet among the trash and the filth. He said to me, "The highest place is always at My feet." I then saw a vision of Jesus laying out a red carpet in our little park, and I saw all of our precious ones walking down the red carpet as our team prayed for them and told them how special they are to the Father.

After the service, I called one of our team members and said, "Go buy a piece of red fabric. We're going to roll out the red carpet at church this week. That Tuesday we laid out the "red carpet" and explained to the people that the red carpet in Hollywood is for honored guests and special people. We told them that they are our honored guests and the special ones. Our team lined up on either side, and one-by-one we hugged them and told them how the Father sees them. About seventy people walked down the red carpet—children in prostitution and abuse, murderers, transvestites, and homeless addicts. Even a few businessmen got in line and received a word from Papa God. When the line had finished, I stepped onto the red carpet—I wasn't going to miss out—and one of our homeless friends, Amilton, put his hand on my head and prayed and prophesied for me. It was beautiful, our most powerful service to date in that little park! The heavens opened up and God's Kingdom came.

After the service, I went to those trees again and said, "I told you so!"

This is what it looks like to love people like Jesus does, selflessly and without an agenda. Often this is one of the hardest parts for us—putting down our own preferences and pride and wholeheartedly embracing the lost. But this is what Jesus did, and this is what it means to answer creation's cry for the sons and daughters of God to stand up. Like Jesus, when we lay aside our desires and agendas in order to really love others, our glory is revealed. As we lay out the red carpet and honor others when they don't deserve it, we are truly becoming like our Father. We are loving like Jesus loved.

Listen and Love

First, let's talk about agendas. We'll get to selflessness later, though as we'll discover, the two usually walk hand-in-hand. Most people view evangelism through the lens of an agenda—getting people saved. Don't get me wrong; getting saved is a really good thing, but if we're loving people with the agenda of getting them saved, our love is false. It won't stand strong in the face of rebellion or set-backs. It will become easily frustrated because the goal isn't relationship, but the salvation prayer. When we act with an agenda, we unconsciously pursue the completion of a goal rather than connection with a person's heart.

I once taught on sonship and compassion at a mission school that is particularly strong in evangelism. They do an amazing job at taking the gospel to the streets in Brazil. Later that night, we were planning to take them to the streets to minister to prostitutes and transvestites. So as I taught, I said, "Tonight, when we go to the streets, you are not allowed to ask if the person is saved, and you can't ask the person to say a 'repeat after me' prayer."

Shock fell over the whole group because that was their mode of operation—to ask people if they know Jesus and, if not, to ask them if they'd like to pray a prayer to receive Jesus. This concept is not necessarily wrong; however, when ministering to the homeless and destitute, it simply doesn't work. Many of the people we minister to are used to being sought out and bought for what they can do. If we start the conversation with an attempt to get something from them—even if it's their acceptance of Jesus—we're still missing the target. The target is their hearts.

I told the students, "Tonight I just want you to look in their eyes, listen, and love. If the Holy Spirit leads you to pray with them, do it. If He leads you to cry with them, go for it. Just follow His leading. Look them in their eyes, listen, and love."

"But what about their eternal life?" one student asked.

"How would you describe eternal life to them?" I asked.

He said, "I would tell them that they can live forever."

"The problem is," I said, "these people don't have any concept of abundant life. Their lives have been filled with sin, pain, and death. They don't see living forever as a good thing."

"To live forever with God," another student shouted.

"Okay," I said. "But many of these people have a negative view of God because they say things like 'Where was God when I was raped as a child?' or 'God let my husband die,' or 'God allowed that pastor to molest me.' Telling them they can live forever with someone they don't like is not very appealing."

The truth is, the answers those students gave were good answers—for people who already have an understanding of who God is. But sometimes we jump the gun and offer eternal life to people before they even know their value to God. When we do that, we make it very clear to them that we have an agenda. Only when we align our focus with God's—in pursuit of their hearts—will we be able to minister to people without an agenda.

Fabiano and Bruna[1]

One night, when we were on the streets in Curitiba, we saw a young woman standing on a corner whom we had never seen before. A few of our girls began talking with her while several of the guys and I went to talk with a few homeless men on the same corner. Her name was Bruna, and we loved her from the minute that we saw her. She was beautiful and full of love with a tender heart. As the girls were talking to her, I saw a man, who I assumed was her pimp, on the other side of the street. He was pacing and watching with a nervous demeanor. I decided to join the girls, to make sure they were safe, and as I did, Bruna asked us to pray for her husband and her. The man across the street, she explained, was her husband, Fabiano.

He came with her to the streets to watch over her. Essentially her husband was her pimp.

She called Fabiano over. After we prayed with both of them, I asked Fabiano how they had gotten into this situation. He began to cry as he told me their story. They have four children, all of them from previous relationships. Fabiano was an Assemblies of God pastor for eight years. While he was pastoring, his first wife was unfaithful, and she left him. One night, she decided to come home to him, and as she walked into their living room, the man she had been unfaithful with followed her in and shot her in the head right in front of Fabiano.

Deeply shaken, he left the ministry and started using and dealing drugs. He was in a violent car accident that should have killed him, but the grace of God left only his right leg badly burned and scarred. Not long after he recovered, he met Bruna, who was twenty-four—fourteen years younger than him. When Bruna was eight years old, her mother had died of complications due to AIDS. Her mother was also a prostitute. We see that generational curse here a lot, and part of our purpose here involves breaking that cycle. Bruna was raped three times as a child, when she was seven, nine, and thirteen. When she was fourteen, she had her first baby. Her first husband was abusive, and after several years of that abuse, she left him. Then she found Fabiano.

After Fabiano and Bruna got together, he was arrested for having a large amount of cocaine in his car. While he was in jail, Bruna started prostituting to pay the bills and provide for the children. When Fabiano got out, they were addicted to the fast money of prostitution and didn't attempt to get permanent jobs. Prostituting is not easy money; it's not easy spiritually, emotionally, or physically, but it is fast money. The minimum wage in Brazil is R$550 per month, and they can make that prostituting in one week. In fact, transvestites can make even more money; they generally make three or four times more than women in prostitution. However, just as the money comes in fast, it goes out fast, too. Fabiano once told me, "I can make R$200 at an honest job, and it lasts us a week, but R$1,000 from the streets lasts a couple of days."

The night that we met Fabiano and Bruna, we got their phone number and told them we'd like to get together. We tried calling them for about two weeks, and they never answered. It's not unusual for us to receive a fake phone number from someone on the streets, but I felt different about this one. Then one night when we were on the streets, we saw Fabiano from a distance. When he saw us, he started to run away, so I asked Aline, one of our staff members, to chase after him. She chased him for about two blocks until he finally stopped. Once I got there, I asked him why he had run away, and he said, "Oh, I wasn't running," Even though he was still out of breath from the chase. Finally, he was honest and admitted he was ashamed to have us at their house because of the life they'd been living. We assured him that we loved them and really wanted to get to know them better. Over the next couple months, we visited their house several times, they visited ours, and we saw them on the streets less and less. We became very close with them.

After a while, they told us they weren't legally married—they had just been living together all this time—but they wanted to get officially married and leave the streets. They asked if we would come to their wedding in a courthouse as witnesses.

We said, "We can do that and even better. If you'll let us, we'd love to provide the photographer and cook the meal for your reception."

A few weeks later, we went to the courthouse and witnessed their wedding. Kate, one of our team members, was the photographer. She even got all of the photos printed in an album because we really wanted it to be special for them. At the reception, which was at their house, several of our team members and I cooked about five pounds of chicken, ten pounds of filet mignon, garlic bread, rice, and beans. We topped it all off with chocolate cake! Every scrap of food was devoured. It was a beautiful site as we served Fabiano and Bruna and their friends. There were family members, friends from the church they had started to attend, children from the local slum, and people from their neighborhood.

After the meal, Fabiano asked if I would lead some worship and share a message. As it rained, we sang a few songs under their carport, and I shared a very simple message. I read from John 2 about the wedding at Cana, the place of Jesus's first miracle. I told them this story is not only about a miracle, but also about transformation. Just as the water had been turned into wine, God was turning the water in their hearts and the water in their family into wine. He was transforming them from the inside out.

With tears in his eyes, Fabiano told his guests, "We have been living on the streets, and we've been lost in such darkness, but one night God found us through these friends here, and when we looked into their eyes, we saw Jesus. I am so thankful that God sent these shepherds to find the lost sheep on the streets of Brazil."

After that, we prayed and prophesied over their marriage and their family. It was such a beautiful night. I felt as though I was walking in the footsteps of Jesus when He was at the wedding in Cana. A few weeks after the wedding, Fabiano and Bruna left the streets for good and started a remodeling business.

This story illustrates what it can look like to patiently walk with people in relationship and to love them without an agenda. As we pursued their hearts and became a tangible experience of Jesus's love for them, their hearts turned toward home. They began to believe the truth about who they really are and where they belong, and they started to live in that reality.

However, as I mentioned before, when we love without agenda, experiences of selflessness are quick to follow. Our relationship with Fabiano and Bruna has been a sometimes painful revelation of what selfless love looks like.

When Love Is Hard

Leaving the streets is just the beginning of recovery and redemption. Many men and women stay in prostitution because of fear of what they will face when they leave this lifestyle. They fear a lack of finances. They fear trusting others when, as prostitutes, they have been paid to be taken advantage of. They also fear facing the deep pain and hurt that lies within their hearts. This is why we tell people that Shores of Grace is not a street ministry but a redemption ministry. The streets are most often just the meeting point—and the easy part. The process after people leave the streets can be, unfortunately, both difficult and heartbreaking. However, it is not our job to redeem people; it's Jesus's job. We just walk with Him and do what we see Him doing as He pours out His love on the hearts of people.

One night, Bruna called us in tears and asked us to come to their house. She and Fabiano had been fighting. They had lost a few clients for their business, and finances were tight. Fabiano was upset and told Bruna she was worth more to him when she was prostituting because at least she was bringing in money. Bruna wanted to leave him, and Fabiano was as prideful as we had ever heard him. I spent the next hour on the phone pleading with him not to force his wife to prostitute—a conversation I never thought I would have. Fortunately, Bruna stood her ground and refused to go to back to the streets.

We were not able to go to their house that day because our car was in the shop. We had been hit two times on the driver's side of the car, and the entire side needed to be repaired at the body shop—which cost us about $2,500. The next day, as we drove to their house, I felt very angry with Fabiano. As a husband, I thought, *How could you tell your wife that she is worth more when she is prostituting?* My flesh wanted to punch Fabiano in the face and tell him to be a man and take care of his wife. I prayed, "Jesus, it's easy for me to love Bruna. She is beautiful and has such an amazing heart. But I am having a really hard time loving Fabiano. Please show me how to love him like You love him."

When we arrived at their house, Fabiano was very hardhearted. His attitude told us he didn't want us to be there. We ate a meal with them, and then Fabiano abruptly said he needed to go to the store. He got into their VW Kombi van and left. A few minutes later, the phone rang. Bruna answered, and I could tell she was nervous as she hung up and began talking to our staff member, Aline. However, I couldn't understand what they were saying.

Then Aline came over to me with a worried look and said, "Please come with me." This seemed strange, but I obliged and followed her out to the street, where she pointed to our car. When Fabiano left, he had backed their van up into our car—the same side that we had just paid $2,500 to repair. Inside, I screamed, "Ahhhhhhhhhh!" However, externally I kept my peace as Aline explained that Fabiano was waiting down the street and would not come home until we left because he was afraid that I would be angry with him.

In that moment, the Lord said to me, "You asked Me to show you how to love Fabiano; here is your opportunity." I've heard it said before that when we pray for courage, God doesn't give us courage, but opportunities in which we can learn to be courageous. Likewise, when we pray for more love, God will give us more opportunities to love. I asked Bruna to call Fabiano and tell him that I was not angry and to come home. He was very nervous when he arrived, and he came and apologized. I just put my arms around him, embraced him, and told him that I love him more than a stupid car and that it was no big deal. God used that moment to break his pride and soften his hard heart.

Jesus will use all of life's situations to teach us how to love like He loves. He loved through all circumstances. He loved Mary when she sat adoringly at His feet, and He loved Judas when he was betraying Him with a kiss. His love truly is unconditional, and the closer I get to Him, the more I realize how conditional my love so often is. Jesus threw out all conditions when He was on the cross. The cross is the perfect picture of unconditional love, which is why Jesus said we need to take up our cross and follow Him. As we allow Jesus to examine our hearts, He will show us the areas where our love is conditional, and He will teach us how to love like He does. He will teach us to love selflessly and without an agenda.

The definition of prostitution is doing for money—or for gain—what we would not do for love. As we began ministering to women in prostitution, I realized that there were areas of my life where I was prostituting love. I sometimes loved people for what they could do for me instead of simply for who they are. We have learned to truly love by being around the beautiful men and women on the streets, because the only love they know has a price, and they deeply desire to know true, unconditional love. They long to be loved for who they are. In reality, we all desire to be loved for who we are, not just for what we can do. This is the pure love Jesus pours out on us, and as we receive it, we get to give it away. We were bought with a song and a kiss. The song that Jesus sang over us was, "It's all for you!"

And with our lives, we get to sing back to Him, "It's all for You!"

Father's Eyes

By Nic and Rachael Billman

You have your Father's eyes and His smile
You have your Father's heart and His favor

You look like your Father
You look like your Father

You wear your Daddy's ring and His garments
You wear your Daddy's cologne and His grace
You look like your Father
You look like Your Father

When the world sees the sons and daughters
They see the eyes of a loving Father
When the lost hears the song of the bride
They hear the sound of the bridegrooms delight

Cause it's Christ in me the hope of glory
Christ in me reveals the Father
Light me on fire and the world will watch me burn
Light me on fire and the world will watch me burn

CHAPTER NINE

Compelled by Love

For the love of Christ compels us, because we judge thus: that if One died for all, then all died; and He died for all, that those who live should live no longer for themselves, but for Him who died for them and rose again.

—2 Corinthians 5:14-15

When I was only seven years old, my parents made the decision to become foster parents for babies with HIV who had little chance of surviving. Within a year, we had two beautiful babies at our house, Tito and Kyra. Tito's mother had left him on his grandmother's door step when he was ten months old. Kyra's mother had abandoned her at the hospital not long after she was born. We all loved them from the minute they arrived in our house. At the time, my dad was a pastor at a wonderful United Methodist Church in a rural area outside of Philadelphia. He had been appointed to that church when my brother was just a baby, and I was born there; it was all we had known.

When my parents brought these two babies home, controversy arose in the church. In the early 1990s, much fear surrounded the subject of HIV and AIDS. At the time, many people believed you could get the virus simply through breath, saliva, or even touch. Some people in the church did not want the babies to come to the church at all; others didn't want to allow them in the same nursery as their children, and others suggested that we construct a separate nursery for babies with HIV. Parents of some of my best friends would not let their kids come to our house anymore, and others would no longer let me go to their homes. People told my parents that they were putting their own children at risk and that it was a big mistake. I watched as some of my parents best friends turned their backs on them and would not support them in this great moment of need.

Though many responded negatively, not all did. Another family in the church also chose to become foster parents for unwanted babies with special needs. Compassion is contagious. When we are around people who are full of the radical compassion of Jesus, we can't help but surrender to the weight of His love. Every other month, we needed to take Tito and Kyra to the children's hospital in Philadelphia to be tested. Several months after we had taken them into our family, Tito's test came back negative. There was no sign of HIV. The next month, Kyra's test also came back negative. Through this healing process, God restored many of the relationships that had been broken, and our church family rejoiced together.

Through it all, I watched, as a young boy, the way in which my parents never wavered in their compassion for or commitment to those two babies. They refused to let the fear of disease or the pressure from other people get in the way of their love. It was a powerful lesson for me about what real love looks like and how easily fear and compromise can get in its way.

Love Is the Center

Essentially, what I learned from my parents is that love must be at the center of everything we do. It must be the motivating force. If it's not, something else will motivate us—usually something ugly like fear or greed. Even our good actions can have impure motives, but the fruit of our actions will tell us the truth about our hearts. As Jesus said, the world will be able to tell that we follow Him when we love the way He loves. Love must always be the center.

Paul the apostle also made this clear when he placed the Love Chapter—First Corinthians 13—right in the middle of two chapters about the spiritual gifts, including prophecy and tongues. Paul was teaching us about what must be found at the center of all the good things we do. In the center of our gifting, at the core of our prophecy, love must shine. Of course, this doesn't just apply to spiritual gifts, but to everything we do. It applies to the way we go about life and the way we interact with the people we meet. And it is stronger than the fears and temptations we encounter along the way. At the close of chapter 13, Paul tells us to abide in faith, hope, and love, highlighting love as the greatest. In this Kingdom of the Abba King, love is the center of all things. Love must be the motive, always.

In a unique way, in our ministry on the streets, we get to choose love over fear on a daily basis. Take, for example, Rayane, a thirteen-year-old pregnant girl and the first child we took into our rescue home. She is a beautiful young woman, and we had seen her often on the streets. At one time, she lived with her mother and seven brothers in a slum, but she ran away to live on the streets because she believed it was safer. The place where we found her is actually the most dangerous section of our city and one of the most dangerous areas of Brazil. Grown homeless men have told us that they avoid this area because of the violence. Murders happen every day. Children as young as eight years old carry knives in their shorts and stab people to death to gain credibility. This is where she felt safer. This was her playground. We planted our first street church in this same area, and Rayane would come and draw pictures, and our girls would paint her nails.

The place where we found Rayane is most people's worst nightmare, yet it is "home" to many children and teenagers who have fled abusive homes. People often tell us to avoid it because of the violence and danger, and on more than one occasion, we have broken up fights and attempted murders. Despite the risk, we go because we are compelled by love and because we believe the light shines in the darkness and the darkness cannot overcome the light (see John 1:5). When we go into the streets, we understand what Jesus meant when He said we are the light of the world (see Matt. 5:14). The light inside us is most fully revealed when we step onto the blackest streets of the world. We need not fear when we are following the lead of His love, a love so great that He never, ever stops calling the names of His lost sons and daughters and seeking them out in the dangerous places. Hearing His heart for the lost and the abandoned, we join in His call. We cannot let fear get in the way of love.

Never Let Fear Get in the Way of Love

John, who is often called the apostle of love, wrote about this very thing: *"Love has been perfected among us in this: that we may have boldness in the day of judgment; because as He is, so are we in this world"* (1 John 4:17). Here John tells us clearly that love has been perfected among us. It has already happened through Jesus, and the result of that love is boldness. It's not something that we need to wait for so that we can be fearless. We already have it because love was perfected when Jesus lived, died, and rose again in perfect love and intimacy with the Father. He did not let fear get in the way of love, even when love meant dying on a cross. In fact, He let love get in the way of fear. Hebrews 12:2 tells us that for the joy that was set before Him, Jesus endured the cross. The restoration of relationship with us was the joy that was set before Him. In His worst moment of pain and suffering, when all had abandoned Him and fear was knocking on His door, Jesus chose to hold onto His love for us. That was what enabled Him to persevere.

In Jesus we see the reality that *"...perfect love casts out fear..."* (1 John 4:18). It worked for Him, and it will work for us. Because Jesus perfected love within us, we can have boldness to love in the same way that He loved, even when love is the more painful or scary choice. This verse goes on to say that there is no fear in love and that whoever fears has not been made perfect in love. Whenever I feel fear creeping in to my decision making, I pray a simple prayer, "Father, please continue to perfect Your love inside of me so I will not let fear get in the way of love." When we live and love as Jesus did, we will let love get in the way of fear.

Believing What Jesus Said

Many Christians are so afraid of sin and the devil that they turn off their love for people and their faith for freedom. Jesus modeled the opposite. He showed us that faith in God's goodness and the experience of His perfect love enables us to risk love in dangerous places. The first step toward fearless love is believing what Jesus said.

In Matthew 16, Jesus asked His disciples who people said He was. They told Him a variety of answers—John the Baptist, Elijah, Jeremiah, or one of the prophets. Then Jesus asked, *"Who do you say that I am?"* (Matt. 16:15).

Peter answered, *"You are the Christ, the Son of the living God"* (Matt. 16:16).

In response, Jesus said:

Blessed are you, Simon Bar-Jonah, for flesh and blood has not revealed this to you, but My Father who is in heaven. And I also say to you that you are Peter, and on this rock I will build My church, and the gates of Hades shall not prevail against it. And I will give you the keys of the kingdom of heaven, and whatever you bind on earth will be bound in heaven, and whatever you loose on earth will be loosed in heaven (Matt. 16:17-19).

When Peter recognized and confessed who Jesus really was, Jesus made a prophetic declaration of Peter's future and the future of the Church. When we believe in Him, He declares what He says we can do. This is what happened with Peter. Then we must choose to not only believe in Jesus—who He is and what He did—but to believe that we are who He says we are and will do what He said we will do. It's easy to believe Jesus worked miracles; it's harder to believe His promise that we will do what He did and even greater (see John 14:12). However, we must not stop short of our destinies. We must not be satisfied with simply believing in Jesus. We must believe His promises, too.

We must believe that the gates of hell will not prevail against us. Many of us spend way too much time empowering a defeated enemy instead of walking in the truth of what Jesus declared over the Church. In this passage, the word Jesus used was *hades*, which means "the place of death."[1] He was declaring to the Church that death will not overcome us because He knew that shortly thereafter He would overcome death.

Many people have read this verse as a defensive statement promising us that the enemy will not be able to harm us. It is just the opposite. Gates do not move around. They do not come knocking on our door to overcome us. Rather, gates are fixed realities that serve to keep something or someone safe inside, to allow passage, and to keep intruders outside. In other words, Jesus was saying, "As you advance the Kingdom even to the gates of hell and death, they will not be able to stand up against you." We must think and live proactively, not reactively. We were not created to live in fear of the enemy and his legions. They have already been defeated, and we walk in the victory that Jesus secured for us. Too often we are not proactive in advancing the Kingdom, but instead live in reaction to the attacks of the enemy. When we do this, we allow fear to be our motivator, not love.

Even in prayer and intercession, we are often too reactive and defensive. I'm not saying that when bad things happen we shouldn't pray. However, I do think we should assume the enemy *will* attack and begin declaring and receiving the promises of the Father in advance. In our cities, instead of praying against the drugs, violence, and crime, we must go to the streets and take the Kingdom of Heaven with us. In our schools, instead of picketing and arguing, we must take the love of the Father to the teachers, administrators, and students. The darkness will not prevail against the advance of our love. After all, we are empowered with the keys to the Kingdom and with the same spirit that raised Christ from the dead. But if we sit back and do nothing, darkness *will* prevail against the lost of our generation.

Actions Speak Louder

Unfortunately, many of us, though we are children of Love Himself, let fear rule in our hearts. We see this regularly as we travel around the United States and Brazil to train people for street ministry. Often people make fearful statements like, "I would try to love the homosexuals, but they make me uncomfortable," or, "What if those people steal from me?" or, "What if I pray for people in the hospital and they aren't healed?" A lot of pastors here in Brazil tell me they fear ministering to the prostitutes in the streets because of how it might look to their people. Similarly, when we lived in Pennsylvania, a friend told me God had put a specific bar on his heart but that he was afraid to go there because people from church might see his car parked outside. In this way, many people have given fear the center spot, allowing it to block the flow of the Father's love through them.

Here's the deal. Fear is very good at coming up with logical reasons for why we should not to go to the places of greatest need. However, the cross was not logical. It was not logical for an innocent man, whose words were substantiated by demonstrations of miraculous power, to be condemned and crucified. It was not logical for that man to go without a fight. The cross was not logical; it was radical. Of course, being radical doesn't mean lacking wisdom. However, God chooses the foolish things to shame the wise and the weak things to shame the strong (see 1 Cor. 1:27). Very often, spiritual wisdom seems foolish to our natural human reasoning. This is because the wisdom of the world operates in logic whereas the wisdom of God operates in love. In the Kingdom, love is always the motive. And God is looking for people with willing hearts and radical compassion who will walk out love in the dark places.

For example, instead of being afraid of what people from your church will think if they see you on the streets, take a few of them with you. Start a street team at your church. Instead of being afraid of people seeing your car at the bar, grab a good Christian brother and go together. If you're afraid to talk to homosexuals because of discomfort, you might need to ask God to examine your heart and help you see what's causing the discomfort. Most likely, the problem is not with them but with you. As you let your Father expose the fears you've believed, His perfect love will empower you to love like He does.

Another excuse I often hear is, "But I don't know what to say." To counteract this fear, we train our staff members that they can prophesy and encourage at any time. When we're on the streets, I often will introduce our team to a woman in prostitution and then say, "Each of our team members has a word from Father God for you; we'll start here with Jonathan." I don't ask my team in advance; I just assume each person will have a word because I know the Father has millions of thoughts for each one of His children (see Ps. 139:17-18), and I know my team members know His voice (see John 10:15-16). Sometimes, we spend so much time worrying about what to say that we forget to just be who we are—sons and daughters who reveal the Father.

Not long ago, I witnessed this truth in a way I will never forget. We were on the streets one night, and we came across a transvestite named Daniel. We had attempted to talk to him many times before, but every time he would walk away or tell us to leave. However, we never stopped gently trying to win his heart. On this night, we were with a spiritual mother of ours, Tracee Looslee. When we encountered Daniel, he was, as usual, disinterested and cold. Daniel has a scar on his face, presumably from a client; many of them have plenty of scars to remind them of the danger of their business. As we were about to walk away, Tracee reached up and put her hand on the scar on Daniel's face and stared into his eyes. Time seemed to stop as they looked into each other's eyes. Tears began to run down Daniel's cheeks as Tracee spoke the Father's love to his heart. That night, he gave us his number and asked us to call him. All our words were ineffective, but simple affection from a mama broke into Daniel's heart and gave him an encounter with the Father's love.

Saint Francis is believed to have said, "Preach the gospel at all times, and if necessary, use words." While many have debated this statement, the simple point is that the demonstration of love through action is more important than the words we choose to describe that love. Many of our mamas have said it this way: "Actions speak louder than words."

Recently, at one of our street churches, we had a couple visitors from another ministry. After worship, we handed out small envelopes and asked people to draw a picture to encourage another person. After they had all drawn their pictures, we gave them each a homemade cookie to put in the envelopes. "Now give your picture and your cookie to another person here to bless them, just as Jesus gave gifts to bless the ones He loves," I said. It was a short activity and quite messy, but in the midst of it, many of the people got the point of sacrifice, giving, and love.

At the end, one of the visitors asked one of our staff members, "Aren't you going to preach or have a sermon?"

"That was the sermon," the staff member said.

Church looks different on the streets—sometimes we have communion with juice boxes and granola bars. If we are diligent about love, our social norms or ideas about what church should look like can get in the way. But we must not let fear of change or the unknown hold us back either. Only love will show people the way back home. For this reason, we chose not to be afraid of what they've been through or the issues they have. We choose not to fear entering their world or speaking their language, because we want to give them a picture of Jesus they can understand. We let love lead, and we let Jesus throw aside any of our misconceptions that get in the way. Through it all, our desire is to reveal the tangible compassion and power of Jesus through our actions—whether we are praying for the sick, drawing a picture from Papa, or just being open arms for the abandoned.

Radical Love

This is the power of radical love. Jesus was a radical lover because He acted against the norms and traditions of the culture for the sake of love. In that culture, people feared lepers, so they sent them away to rot in isolation. But Jesus put His hands on the lepers and cleansed them. In that culture, harlots were used by men for selfish pleasure and then stoned when they needed someone to blame. Jesus embraced the harlots, loved them purely, and called them friends. In that culture, rabbis maintained a sense of dignity and self-imposed honor, even to the point of snobbery. Jesus took off His outer garments and washed the feet of His servants. In that culture, many rules and laws told people what they could and could not do and when. Jesus broke the rules—all in the name of love.

Today darkness is covering the earth and deep darkness is covering the people. Everywhere we look we see lust, perversion, immorality, prostitution, and abuse. The giant of sexual perversion is not a sleeping giant; he is roaming to and fro throughout the earth seeking for those he may devour. This is the hour for the sons and daughters of God to arise and shine, because our light has already come. His glory will arise and be seen upon us. Even kings and government leaders will be attracted to His light upon our lives because Jesus is the desire of the nations. Do not fear. This is good news! His light shines brightest in the darkness. Right here, in the middle of the darkness of our generation, is the perfect place for the sons and daughters of God to arise. The Father invites us to take a walk with Him on the streets of this world and to plant gardens as we go.

Come Find Me

By Nic Billman

When I was hungry, you gave Me bread.
When I was thirsty, you gave Me a drink.
When I was sick, you came to Me.
When I was naked and poor, you clothed Me in grace.

Just stare into the eyes of the child who's left alone.
There you'll find Me, there you'll find Me.
Just open up your arms to hold the least of these.
There'll you find Me, there you'll find Me.
Come find Me.

I was in prison, you came to see Me.
I was broken, you made Me whole.
I was abandoned, you gave Me a home.
I was wounded, you healed Me with love.

CHAPTER TEN

Come Find Me

"Come, you blessed of My Father, inherit the kingdom prepared for you from the
foundation of the world: for I was hungry and you gave me food; I was thirsty and you
gave me drink; I was a stranger and you took me in; I was naked and you clothed me;
I was sick and you visited me; I was in prison and you came to me."

—Matthew 25:34-36

y very first trip to Brazil was in October of 2008. I saw God do
many miracles and heal many people on that trip. One of my
favorite stories from that trip is that of a little boy named Julio. When I saw
Julio and his mother standing a few people back in the line, I asked the
translator to bring them to the front. I had been away from my children for
ten days, and I was really missing them. I wanted to pray with this young
boy. Julio's mother explained that he was four years old and had been born
eighty percent deaf in both ears. I asked her to demonstrate the volume in
which she would have to speak for him to hear her. She had to yell loudly
to get his attention. They had prayed many times for his healing, and yet
when I asked the mother if she believed for his healing, she said yes without
hesitation. I got down on my knees and put my hands over Julio's ears. I felt
the gift of faith rising up within me, and I simply said, "Julio, Jesus loves you.
Jesus loves you."

As soon as I said it the second time, he took a quick deep breath, and
his head popped up. He jumped into his mother's arms, and she whispered,
"I love you."

With a huge smile on his face, he whispered back, "I love you, Mama." Not only was his hearing restored, but the speech impairment he had as a result of the deafness was also healed.

The next day, we had the morning off, and I was resting in the hotel room while most of the team was out shopping for souvenirs or sight-seeing. The room was getting hot, so I walked over to open the window. Outside, I saw a boy laying on a piece of cardboard on the sidewalk. I felt drawn to him. Knowing he would be hungry, I searched my room for anything I had to give him. All I found was a bottle of water, cherry Pop Tarts, and a pack of Shock Tarts. As you can see, at the time I was really on a health food kick. I took the portable feast downstairs and brought it to the boy. He probably weighed about seventy pounds. His whole body was dirty, and his feet were raw and cut open. He spoke no English, and I, at the time, spoke no Portuguese. I was able to figure out that his name was Henrique, but that was about it.

We spent one hour together, there on the dirty sidewalk with no spoken language, only love and friendship. After the hour, I went and found a translator in the hotel lobby, and he helped me find out some information. I learned that Henrique was fifteen years old, and he had been abandoned by his parents when he was ten. He told me about his life and experiences. As I sat listening, I thought, *This is Jesus. I am communing with Jesus.* It was a powerful encounter. We went to a store and bought him some socks and shoes, and despite all of the healings I saw on that trip, my favorite memory was watching Henrique walk away, staring proudly at his shoes.

A couple days later, we were preparing to leave that city to head north to Brasilia. While I was in the hotel lobby, Henrique came to the front door, and one of my team members, a translator, and I went out to meet him. He excitedly told me, "I have a place to sleep tonight!" We congratulated him on his find. He said "I want to show you where I will sleep tonight." We walked with him around the corner, where the dumpsters for the hotel were located. He climbed up over some built-in fencing and dropped down into the garbage of the hotel—my garbage. He had a huge smile on his face as he said, "I have a place to sleep tonight!"

After we said good-bye, I began to cry; my heart was broken because I didn't know what to do. As we rode on the bus to the next city, the Lord spoke to me. He said, "Nic, when I used you to heal the deaf boy and when you bought shoes for the street boy, it's the same to me. It's worship unto the Father." What a great privilege it is to find Jesus in the lost and broken children of the streets—in the least of these—and to pour out my love at His feet.

Come Find Me

One night before we moved to Brazil, we were in our church worshipping with a group of friends. All of us were singing spontaneously in that place of high praise. As I was singing, "Holy, holy, holy," the Lord took me into an open vision. For me, the vision occurred in Brazil because that is where my heart is, but it applies to any geographical location. He took me into a large church in Brazil that was full of people singing and dancing. It was a beautiful and alive church! The people in the church were crying out, "We want to see Your face; we want to hear Your voice; we want to see You!" over and over again. As I watched, I could feel their passion for God filling the room.

Then, all of a sudden, the Holy Spirit took me out to the streets, and I saw hungry children begging for money, a widow sitting alone weeping, a prostitute selling her body, and a drug addict shooting up heroine. From their mouths, I heard the voice of the Lord, "Then come find Me."

Suddenly, I was back in the church, and the people were still crying out, "We want to see Your face; we want to hear Your voice; we want to see You!"

Quickly, I was back to the streets again, and the voice of the Lord again came from the lost and broken, "Come find Me."

So many believers cry out for more of Jesus from within the four walls of the church; all the while, He is inviting us to come out to the streets and find Him in the least of these. This isn't a popular message, but the truth is that Jesus cares very much about His children seeking out and caring for the hurting and broken people in this world. In fact, in Matthew 25, Jesus tells us that at the Final Judgment, when He separates the sheep from the goats, the deciding factor between the two groups will not be how many miracles were done, how big our churches were, or how many people we led in a salvation prayer. No, the determining factor will be whether or not we were able to recognize Jesus in the least of these and whether we cared for the poor and the weary. The genuineness of our relationship with Him will be evident in whether or not we were compelled to love like He loved.

In Matthew 25:34-40, Jesus says to those on His right,

> Then the King [Jesus] will say to those on His right hand, "Come, you blessed of My Father, inherit the kingdom prepared for you from the foundation of the world: for I was hungry and you gave me food; I was thirsty and you gave me drink; I was a stranger and you took me in; I was naked and you clothed me; I was sick and you visited me; I was in prison and you came to me."

> Then the righteous will answer Him saying, "Lord when did we see You hungry and feed You, or thirsty and give You drink? When did we see You a stranger and take You in, or naked and clothe You? Or when did we see You sick or in prison and come to You?"

> And the King will answer and say to them, "Assuredly I say to you, inasmuch as you did it to one of the least of these My brethren, you did it to Me."

Here, Jesus gives us a key to encountering Him. If we want to see Jesus, we will find Him with the hungry and the thirsty. If you want to meet with Jesus, we should seek Him in hospitals and prisons. Of course, as we talked about in the last chapter, living this way is only possible when we refuse to let fear get in the way of love. The Bible promises that when we seek Jesus with all our hearts, we will find Him (see Jer. 29:13). He's given us a clue. We will find Him among the broken.

To those who do, Jesus will say, "Come you who are blessed by My Father and receive your inheritance." The people on the left will have quite a different experience. These are the people who have guarded their earthly inheritance so closely that they have not recognized Jesus among the hungry, the thirsty, the stranger, the naked, the sick, or the prisoner. To these people, Jesus will say, "Depart from me, you cursed, into the everlasting fire prepared for the devil and his angels" (Matt. 25:41). Here's the bottom line: If we truly love Jesus and follow Him, we will care about the same things that He cares about. Our hearts will break for the things that break His heart, and we will desire to be the solution, not just those who point out the problem. The truth is, Jesus is all around us; if we have eyes to see Him, we will.

We can testify to this truth. We have encountered Jesus in deep and amazing ways by caring about the Father's lost children. And we have learned so much from the poor and weary on the streets of Brazil. Many nights we head to the streets or to a rescue home with the expectation that we will teach them about Jesus. Most often, Jesus teaches us through their brokenness and simple desire for true love. It is always a great occurrence when we are sharing with a prostitute or a transvestite and the Father begins to teach us through that person's story. Then the prostitute or transvestite is the one hugging us and sometimes praying for us as we cry under the weight of His love. This sort of "holy switcharoo" has happened many times during our two years on the streets.

The truth is that there is an encounter with Jesus that you can only experience among the least of these. That's not to say that you can't encounter him in other ways and places; of course you can. However, we discover a greater understanding of the depth of His love when we stare into the eyes of the poor and we see Him there.

Communion on the Streets

One of the ways in which we find Jesus in the broken is by relating to them in the way that He did. Jesus always explained the Kingdom in ways that people understood, in parables and stories they could relate to. We like to follow His example. When we arrive at our street church, the people invite us to sit with them, usually offering cardboard for the girls to sit on. This is their grid for fellowship. During worship, I like to tell them, "When we worship God, it's just like when we come to visit, and you are so welcoming, and you invite us to sit with you. When we worship, it's like inviting Papa God to come and sit with us. He isn't looking for big fancy buildings; He's looking for hearts that say, 'Here's a place for You, Papa!'

And He loves to come and visit us right here on the streets." It's one of my favorite things, to watch people gain a simple child-like understanding of worship that will tear down the walls of rejection, abandonment, and fear in their hearts.

During worship, we all draw pictures, and we explain what it is to give an offering—that an offering is not simply a monetary gift, but giving of the heart. It is amazing to watch a person who seemingly has nothing to give excitedly draw a picture and then give it to another person. One night after this time of giving, I taught about communion, explaining that Jesus came not only to die for our sins, but to show us how to live. I told them that Jesus came from Heaven to earth and spent most of His time on the streets with people just like us so that we would know how much He loves us. He chose to be broken and poured out so that we can live abundantly with Him, and when He rose again, it sealed the promise that He will never leave us. Then I took the bread and broke it and passed it to the twenty people in attendance. Then I passed the grape juice, and they all partook of communion that night. Afterward, I brought out some sandwiches and explained that one of Jesus's favorite things to do was to share a meal with the ones He loved. I told them, "These sandwiches are a sign of the promise of Jesus, that He has never left you."

Because we have our services out in the open at the park, hundreds of people are always nearby. We start every week by walking around the park and praying for the sick. When someone is healed, we share the testimony with the crowd and ask if anyone else needs healing. One night we were praying for a man who had several metal screws in his foot and ankle because a motorcycle had run over his foot. He also had a problem with his left shoulder that prevented him from lifting his arm above his chest. On this night, my son Forrest was with us; as he and Rachael prayed for the man's foot, the man started to move it around. He turned to his friend sitting next to him and excitedly said, "I can move my foot! I couldn't do that before. It's impossible!"

He got up and started walking around to test it out. All of the pain had left, and total movement was restored. He was so happy he started to dance right there in the park; as he danced, he lifted his hands up and realized his shoulder had been healed as well. He told everyone around what God had done. A man who heard his testimony asked us to pray for his hearing. I asked the man who had been healed to help us pray. When we prayed, the second man's hearing issue was healed as well. It really is that simple. When we seek Him, we'll find Him. When we seek Him among the least of these, not only do we find Him, but His love and power are revealed for all to see.

Love looks like something. In this book I've talked a lot about what compassion looks like in our hearts and how it causes us to treat people. This is our starting place, the foundation upon which love grows, and the result of real love for people on the streets is food and clothing for the poor and healing for the hurting. In our work here on the streets of Brazil, we run into two different kinds of Christian groups. One group desires to operate in great love; they constantly take food and clothing to homeless and perform beautiful acts of kindness in the name of Jesus. However, this group tends to skip the power aspect of the Kingdom, rarely praying for healing or miracles. The other group goes to the streets desiring to operate in power; they pray for miracles and healings, and at times they see great fruit. However, the hungry are left unfed and the naked unclothed. The answer is found in the balance of the two.

In Scripture, we see no better example of ministry to the poor than in Stephen, who was chosen to help with the distribution of food for the widows and orphans because he was a man full of faith and the Holy Spirit (see Acts 6:5-6). As he distributed food to the poor, he moved in great power and performed many miracles. In other words, Stephen didn't just say, "Here's a cheeseburger" to the hungry. He said, "Here's a cheeseburger. In Jesus's name, you are healed. Now get up and walk." We must walk in this same combination of power and love. Feed the hungry, and heal the sick. Clothe the naked, and cleanse the lepers. Love the unloved, and raise the dead. Give water to the thirsty, and cast out the demons. This is the message of the Kingdom. It's what Jesus did when He first walked the streets and announced the Kingdom, and He invites us to find Him there again.

The Father's Love Letter

One cold night in April, I learned two very important truths as I answered Jesus's call to come to the streets. If we want to love the least of these, we must learn them well. Here's how it happened.

As we often do, we took roses and The Father's Love Letter to people on the streets in Curitiba. On this particular night, I felt really desperate for accurate prophetic words. As we went from person to person, I really pressed in internally for prophetic words. I got a few, but nothing that opened up the heavens, at least not to the natural eye. Around 2 a.m., we approached two transvestites on a corner and presented them with the roses and the letters. I had nothing to say; I was stuck. We simply asked if they wanted prayer, they politely obliged, and then we continued on our walk. A block later, we encountered an eleven-year-old girl who was out prostituting. As we shared with her, she remained distant, and it seemed like she was on drugs. She accepted the rose and the letter, but then had to go.

We walked back around the block, and on the corner where we had encountered the two transvestites, we saw their two roses, thrown onto the street and run over by cars. My heart was broken as we drove home that night. I thought, *Father, they don't know! They don't know how valuable they are!* By the time I laid down in my bed, it was about 4 a.m., and I felt deeply frustrated and helpless. I began to pray, "Father, I don't understand. We're going like You said to go, and I'm trying to get words, and nothing is happening."

After some silence, the Father responded, "I didn't tell you that you needed prophetic words. I just told you to look them in the eye and to love them." Instantly, I realized that the whole night I had been so focused on getting words for these men and women that I hadn't looked them in the eyes and listened to their hearts. Because I felt overwhelmed by the pain of their situations, I had subconsciously begun grasping after a quick-fix, like a prophetic word that would instantly transform their lives. As a result, I had neglected love. And in doing so, I had missed the real source of breakthrough. Often the key needed to unlock the hearts of the captives will be revealed in the words that come from their own mouths. We just need to take the time to look and listen.

A few nights later, we were back on the streets, and I was simply listening to these men and women. I was looking them in the eye as a

Father would. I would tell them things like, "I'm so sorry that you have been through that situation. The Father loves you so much, and He wants to restore your heart and redeem dreams inside of you." It was a powerful night, as much for my own learning as for anyone else. Toward the end of the night, we saw those same two transvestites again, and they had a new friend with them. We gave the new one a rose, and as I was handing him the letter, one of the other transvestites pulled his letter from the other night out of his purse and said, "You have to read that! It is so beautiful! I've read mine over and over again." We then prayed with each of them and told them how their Father sees them. It was beautiful!

Here's what I learned. As we go to the streets, we must listen and love. We must see like Jesus sees and pour out our hearts in compassion. Then, we must offer the seeds of love that we've sown in the hearts of the broken as worship to our Father. He's the only one who can make them grow. If we look only with our human eyes, ministry on the streets can sometimes be desperately discouraging. But many times we don't know what God does with the seeds that we plant. Even when the gifts that we give are thrown to the ground and trampled, He still finds a way to water the seeds that were planted in the hearts of the lost.

A Heart for the Nations

With this confidence, let's fully embrace the call of Jesus to find Him in the least of these. Like children who want to be just like their Papa, let's join Him on His walk through the streets of the nations. Let's be like my ten-year-old son Forrest. One night I was out on the streets very late, until about three o'clock in the morning. When I arrived home, I found a notebook sitting on the couch with a note for me on top. The note said,

> Dad,
> Here is my book's first chapter. Can you read it and let me know what you think?
> Love, Forrest

Here is what he wrote:

Chapter One: My Heart For Nations

My heart is for Nepal, Asia, or I will just stay in Brazil, one of them, or all of them. God told me, "Like the sound of the ocean in a shell, you are the sound of My heart for the nations." My heart for Brazil is to stop prostitution. My heart for Asia is to stop the believing in idols, and my heart for Nepal is to tell the poor that they are already rich. God says love each other, so that is what I will do. I will go to nations and love the unloved. When I say that those three are what my heart is for, that does not mean that those are the only countries that I will go to."

There it is—the simple gospel of love overflowing from our hearts to bring the nations home to Papa. "Like the sound of the ocean in a shell, you are the sound of My heart for the nations." This is His invitation to us. We get to be the song of His heart calling His lost ones home. We get to plant flowers in the streets.

I believe a true revival is coming from the dirtiest and most broken places of our generation. It will not be a social justice movement, but a revival of the arts, creativity, and healing that rises up from the streets, the slums, and the poor. A great harvest awaits us in the world. The dry bones are beginning to rattle in the wind. And His voice calls out to us from the poorest and darkest places, saying, "Come find me!" The Father is calling us by name, saying, "Take my hand. Let's walk together. Come walk with me through the garden of this world, through the streets you live on."

Jesus is walking among the poor, the broken, and the lost, and we were created to follow His footprints through the garden. We have much work to do, much love to give. All of creation is groaning and waiting for the revealing of the children of God, for the unveiling of the true identities of the desperate and needy. The Father has hidden His treasure among the lost, the sick, and the broken, and it is our privilege—our glory—to seek out that treasure with Him (see Prov. 25:2). As in the very beginning, once again He is calling His sons and daughters by name, inviting us to walk with Him through the garden of life—between the flowers and the broken.

Closing Declaration

I pray this book has been a blessing and a challenge to you. In conclusion, here is a declaration you can say over your life, your family, your church, and the people you reveal the Father to. It comes right from Isaiah 61, which talks about the anointing of Christ. The word *Christ* means "the anointed one"; being a Christian means being a follower of the Anointed One, or "little anointed ones." This passage in Isaiah not only speaks about the anointing, but also reveals the character of Jesus, which is the heart of God. The purpose of the anointing on our lives is to reveal the character of Jesus, and character sustains the anointing.

I (We) Declare:
The Spirit of God, the Master, is on me (us) because God anointed me (us).
He sent me (us) to preach good news to the poor,
To heal the heartbroken,
To announce freedom to all captives,
To pardon all prisoners.
God sent me (us) to announce the year of His favor—
A celebration of God's destruction of our enemies—
And to comfort all who mourn,
To care for the needs of all who mourn in Zion,
To give them bouquets of roses instead of ashes,
Messages of joy instead of news of doom,
A praising heart instead of a languid spirit.
Rename them "Oaks of Righteousness,"

Planted by God to display His glory.
They'll rebuild the old ruins,
Raise a new city out of the wreckage.
They'll start over on the ruined cities,
Take the rubble left behind and make it new.
You'll hire outsiders to herd your flocks
And foreigners to work your fields,
But you'll have the title "Priests of God,"
Honored as ministers of our God.
You'll feast on the bounty of nations,
You'll bask in their glory.
Because you got a double dose of trouble
And more than your share of contempt,
Your inheritance in the land will be doubled,
And your joy go on forever.
(Isaiah 61:1-7 modified from The Message Bible)

Activations

Activation #1

Take some time to meditate on Ephesians 1:3-14, John 17:3, Galatians 4:6, and Romans 8:15-17. Read each Scripture, declare the truths of each one over your life, and then listen for the Father. Write a letter declaring your sonship and the love that the Father has for you. You may write from what you heard the Father speak, or you may simply write the truth that you received from these Scriptures. Take your letter and share it with someone you trust, and then, just as you've freely received, freely give. Declare the same Scriptures and truths over that person.

Note: You may hear God's voice audibly, you may have an impression, you may feel His presence physically, or you may be filled with peace. God is more than a feeling, and we must not limit Him to human emotions and feelings. However, He will use those things to reveal His presence to us.

Activation #2

In the back of this book, in Appendix 1, is a document titled, "The Father's Love Letter," written by my friend Barry Adams. It is a beautiful letter taken from dozens of Scriptures about the Father's love. We often hand this letter out on the streets to women in prostitution, and we have seen the walls of rejection and fear broken down as they read the letter. Take some time to read through the letter, and let it soak into your heart. You may want to read it several times. Allow the Father to speak to your heart, and receive His love for you. Once you have finished, write a response to the Father from your heart—a love letter to Papa from His child.

I also encourage you to pray and ask the Father to show you a person who really needs a revelation of His love. Then, give them a copy of the letter. You can find it online at www.fatherslovelette.com. It is available in over ninety different languages, and there is even a kids' version. On their site, they also have a video version of the Father's Love Letter that is equally beautiful and powerful.

Activation #3

Play "Where's Jesus" this week at church or at a mall, park, or other public place. Remember, to enter the Kingdom of Heaven, we have to come as children. Just like Leila does, close your eyes and ask Jesus to show you where He is or where He is needed. Open your eyes and listen for His voice. You may receive a word of knowledge about healing. You may receive a word of encouragement for someone. You may just see an obvious need, like a lonely person, a widow, or a person in need. Go be Jesus to that person. Trust in the Father; He will show you the way and provide opportunities for you to reveal His love to those in need.

Activation #4

Are there areas of religion or false belief in your heart that might be blinding compassion and keeping you from your own freedom and joy? Take a moment and allow the Holy Spirit to reveal any such areas in which you may need forgiveness and repentance. God is a good Father; He doesn't get angry with us when we confess areas of pride, but rather He rejoices with each step of our transformation.

Ask the Father to show you people you have seen as lost-cause sinners instead of sons or daughters in waiting. Ask Him to show you people you have labeled as "religious" instead of as children. Then ask the Father to show you how He sees them and how He loves them. After you have received some freedom and revelation in this area, think of a way that you can be a friend and reveal the Father to the people He showed you.

For example, if you discovered that you have been judgmental toward a pastor in your community, or even your own pastor, schedule a time to sit down with that pastor. Ask for forgiveness, and encourage the pastor with the things the Father showed you about the pastor. Chances are, that pastor has been receiving judgment from others as well, and you could be a humble vessel of healing.

Or perhaps you discovered that you have been judgmental or prejudicial toward a homosexual man or woman. Give that person a call or send a letter asking forgiveness. You could also ask forgiveness on behalf of the Church for any hurtful things that have been said or done to that person. Then share with that person, with purity of heart, how the Father loves that person and anything He showed you about that person's heart. Loving and forgiving does not mean agreeing with homosexuality. Jesus died on the cross, not to agree with our sin, but to overcome it. Yet it is the kindness of the Father that leads us to repentance (see Rom. 2:4).

Activation #5

Here are several ideas for how to activate what you've learned in this chapter:

1. Gather a small group of Christian brothers and sisters and pray together for words of knowledge for healing, prophetic words, and words of encouragement. Pick a location to go and share these words—perhaps a mall, a park, or another public place.
2. Go to a hospital or elderly care center and ask for permission to pray for the sick.
3. Go to a street in your city that has prostitutes or strip clubs and hand out roses and The Father's Love Letter.
4. For Valentine's Day, draw love cards from Papa God and take them to a public place to give. For Christmas, draw Christmas cards with prophetic words for the upcoming new year.
5. Rent a private room at a nice restaurant, and invite a woman in prostitution or a dancer to come to a banquet. Have a healthy father figure there to share about the Father's love. It's okay to invite more than one. If you are inviting women in prostitution, offer to pay for their time.
6. Hand out food to the homeless, pray for healing, and prophesy the Father's love for them. Or prepare a special meal and invite a

homeless man or woman to your home for dinner.

Note: In all of these cases, we always suggest that you grab another person or two to go with you. If you don't know where to find people in prostitution in your city or town, share your purpose with the local police and ask if they can point you in the right direction.

Activation #6

Make a list of your comfort zones in ministry; then make a list of things outside your normal. In prayer, submit them to the Lord. Then create an opportunity to step out of your comfort zone and overcome your fears. For example, grab a Christian friend and go together to pray for a stranger at the supermarket or in a restaurant. A good way to practice boldness is to offer to pray for your server when you're out to eat. You can simply say, "We are about to pray for our meal; is there anything we can pray for you for as well?" Eighty percent of the time, people will say yes, or it will at least strike up curiosity and brighten their day. Go step out into your radical and reveal the Father's heart as a son or daughter!

APPENDIX ONE

The Father's Love Letter

My Child,

You may not know me, but I know everything about you.
–Psalm 139:1

I know when you sit down and when you rise up.
–Psalm 139:2

I am familiar with all your ways.
–Psalm 139:3

Even the very hairs on your head are numbered.
–Matthew 10:29-31

For you were made in my image.
–Genesis 1:27

In me you live and move and have your being.
–Acts 17:28

For you are my offspring.
–Acts 17:28

I knew you even before you were conceived.
–Jeremiah 1:4-5

I chose you when I planned creation.
–Ephesians 1:11-12

You were not a mistake, for all your days are written in my book.
–Psalm 139:15-16

I determined the exact time of your birth and where you would live.
–Acts 17:26

You are fearfully and wonderfully made.
–Psalm 139:14

I knit you together in your mother's womb.
–Psalm 139:13

And brought you forth on the day you were born.
–Psalm 71:6

I have been misrepresented by those who don't know me.
–John 8:41-44

I am not distant and angry, but am the complete expression of love.
–1 John 4:16

And it is my desire to lavish my love on you.
–1 John 3:1

. Simply because you are my child and I am your Father.
–1 John 3:1

I offer you more than your earthly father ever could.
–Matthew 7:11

For I am the perfect father.
–Matthew 5:48

Every good gift that you receive comes from my hand.
–James 1:17

For I am your provider and I meet all your needs.
–Matthew 6:31-33

My plan for your future has always been filled with hope.
–Jeremiah 29:11

Because I love you with an everlasting love.
–Jeremiah 31:3

My thoughts toward you are countless as the sand on the seashore.
–Psalm 139:17-18

And I rejoice over you with singing.
–Zephaniah 3:17

I will never stop doing good to you.
–Jeremiah 32:40

For you are my treasured possession.
–Exodus 19:5

I desire to establish you with all my heart and all my soul.
–Jeremiah 32:41

And I want to show you great and marvelous things.
–Jeremiah 33:3

If you seek me with all your heart, you will find me.
–Deuteronomy 4:29

Delight in me and I will give you the desires of your heart.
–Psalm 37:4

For it is I who gave you those desires.
–Philippians 2:13

I am able to do more for you than you could possibly imagine.
–Ephesians 3:20

For I am your greatest encourager.
–2 Thessalonians 2:16-17

I am also the Father who comforts you in all your troubles.
–2 Corinthians 1:3-4

When you are brokenhearted, I am close to you.
–Psalm 34:18

As a shepherd carries a lamb, I have carried you close to my heart.
–Isaiah 40:11

One day I will wipe away every tear from your eyes.
–Revelation 21:3-4

And I'll take away all the pain you have suffered on this earth.
–Revelation 21:3-4

I am your Father, and I love you even as I love my son, Jesus.
–John 17:23

For in Jesus, my love for you is revealed.
–John 17:26 .

He is the exact representation of my being.
–Hebrews 1:3

He came to demonstrate that I am for you, not against you.
–Romans 8:31

And to tell you that I am not counting your sins.
–2 Corinthians 5:18-19

Jesus died so that you and I could be reconciled.
–2 Corinthians 5:18-19

His death was the ultimate expression of my love for you.
–1 John 4:10

I gave up everything I loved that I might gain your love.
–Romans 8:31-32

If you receive the gift of my son Jesus, you receive me.
–1 John 2:23

And nothing will ever separate you from my love again.
–Romans 8:38-39

Come home and I'll throw the biggest party heaven has ever seen.
–Luke 15:7

I have always been Father, and will always be Father.
–Ephesians 3:14-15

My question is...Will you be my child?
—John 1:12-13

I am waiting for you.
—Luke 15:11-32

Love, Your Dad (Almighty God)

APPENDIX TWO

The Heart of an Orphan; The Heart of a Son[1]

The Heart of an Orphan		The Heart of a Son
See God as Master	IMAGE OF GOD	See God as a loving Father
Independent / Self-reliant	DEPENDENCY	Interdependent / Acknowledges Need
Live by the Love of Law	THEOLOGY	Live by the Law of Love
Insecure / Lack peace	SECURITY	Rest and Peace
Strive for the praise, approval, and acceptance of man	NEED FOR APPROVAL	Totally accepted in God's love and justified by grace
A need for personal achievement as you seek to impress God and others, or no motivation to serve at all	MOTIVE FOR SERVICE	Service that is motivated by a deep gratitude for being unconditionally loved and accepted by God
Duty and earning God's favor or no motivation at all	MOTIVE BEHIND CHRISTIAN DISCIPLINES	Pleasure and delight
"Must" be holy to have God's favor, thus increasing a sense of shame and guilt	MOTIVE FOR PURITY	"Want to" be holy; do not want anything to hinder intimate relationship with God
Self-rejection from comparing yourself to others	SELF-IMAGE	Positive and affirmed because you know you have such value to God
Seek comfort in counterfeit affections: addictions, compulsions, escapism, busyness, hyper-religious activity	SOURCE OF COMFORT	Seek times of quietness and solitude to rest in the Father's presence and love
Competition, rivalry, and jealousy toward others' success and position	PEER RELATIONSHIPS	Humility and unity as you value others and are able to rejoice in their blessings and success
Accusation and exposure in order to make yourself look good by making others look bad	HANDLING OTHERS' FAULTS	Love covers as you seek to restore others in a spirit of love and gentleness

See authority as a source of pain; distrustful toward them and lack a heart attitude of submission	VIEW OF AUTHORITY	Respectful, honoring; you see them as ministers of God for good in your life
Difficulty receiving admonition; you must be right so you easily get your feelings hurt and close your spirit to discipline	VIEW OF ADMONITION	See the receiving of admonition as a blessing and need in your life so that your faults and weaknesses are exposed and put to death
Guarded and conditional; based upon others' performance as you seek to get your own needs met	EXPRESSION OF LOVE	Open, patient, and affectionate as you lay your life and agendas down in order to meet the needs of others
Conditional & Distant	SENSE OF GOD'S PRESENSE	Close & Intimate
Bondage	CONDITION	Liberty
Feel like a Servant/Slave	POSITION	Feel like a Son/Daughter
Spiritual ambition; the earnest desire for some spiritual achievement and distinction and the willingness to strive for it; a desire to be seen and counted among the mature.	VISION	To daily experience the Father's unconditional love and acceptance and then be sent as a representative of His love to family and others.
Fight for what you can get!	FUTURE	Sonship releases your inheritance!

APPENDIX THREE

Law vs. Grace Chart

Luke 6:35-38

Law	Grace
What Is Right & Fair	**An Undeserved Gift**
Satan Traffics In Law	**God Traffics In Grace**
Satan Is The Prosecutor	**Jesus Is Our Advocate**
Satan Is Negative	**God Is Positive**
Negative Thoughts	Positive Thoughts
The Accuser Of The Brethren	The Holy Spirit-The Comforter
The Accuser Accuses	The Comforter Comforts
Ephesians 4:26,27/Galatians 5:19-21	Ephesians 4:29-32/Galatians 5:22,23

Galatians 6:7,8

Law	Grace
If You Sow Judgment...	**If You Sow Grace...**
Accusatory Thoughts & Words	Edifying Thoughts & Words
Criticism	Encouragement
Fault Finding/Blaming Others	Seeing Own Fault First
Demands Rights	Yields Rights
Demands Justice	Pronounces Innocence
Rehearses Wounds	Releases Wounds
Unforgiveness & Bitterness	Forgiveness & Love
Rejects & Devalues Others	Accepts & Values Others
...You Reap The Law And Release A Self-Imposed Curse	**...You Reap Grace And Release God's Blessing**
Psalm 109:17-19,29	1 Peter 3:9-13
Resentment & Bitterness	Innocence Restored
Hardness & Anger	Gentleness & Meekness
Walls - Heart Of Stone	Transparency/Openness
Unforgiving Relationships	Forgiving Relationships
Pride	Humility
Bondage	Liberty
Anxiety/Stress Related Disease	Rest/Peace/Divine Health
Wounded/Shattered Life	Healing/Wholeness
There Is No Love In Law	**Mercy Triumphs Over Judgment**
Rom 7:5	James 2:13

Notes

Chapter 3

[1] See Appendix 1 for a copy of The Father's Love Letter.

Chapter 4

[1] Kevin Prosch and Heidi Baker, "The Gift," audio recording, *The Gift* (2009), track 1. Quoted with permission from Kevin Prosch.

[2] *Merriam-Webster's Dictionary Online*, s.v. "Prodigal."

Chapter 5

[1] Heidi Baker, interview with Turning Point International, accessed August 30, 2012, http://www.turningpointzone.com/heidi-baker-compelled-by-love.

[2] Randy Clark teaches people, as they pray for healing, to ask people whether any areas of unforgivness or any history with witchcraft or the occult exist in their lives. Many times when we are praying for healing, when we get to that question, the true issue is revealed. Even doctors confirm that bitterness and unforgiveness can cause physical disease or discomfort.

[3] *Strong's Exhaustive Concordance*, s.v. "Ginosko" (Greek #1097).

Chapter 6

[1] Quoted with permission from Randy Clark.

Chapter 8

[1] Not their real names.

Chapter 9

[1] Strong's Exhaustive Concordance, s.v. "Hades" (Greek #86).

Appendix 1

[1] "The Father's Love Letter," used by permission of Father Heart Communications © 1999-2011. www.FathersLoveLetter.com.

Appendix 2

[1] Jack and Trisha Frost, Shiloh Place Ministries, www.shilohplace.org. Used by permission.